SEMIOTIC AND COGNITIVE STUDIES

XI
THE FUTURE OF MEMORY

SEMIOTIC AND COGNITIVE STUDIES

XI

SERIES EDITORS
UMBERTO ECO
and
PATRIZIA VIOLI

THE FUTURE OF MEMORY

EDITED BY

GIULIO BLASI

CONTRIBUTORS:

GIULIO BLASI
PATRICK BAZIN
RICCARDO RIDI
MICHELE SANTORO
PAOLO CIANCARINI
MICHELA SAVIANE
BRUCE STERLING
FABIO VITALI
ANDREA BABICH
SEAMUS ROSS

BREPOLS

Editing and pagination by Horizons Unlimited (Bologna, Italy).

© Brepols Turnhout 2002

All rights reserved. No part of this publication may be reproduced, stored in
a retrieval system, or transmitted, in any form or by any means, electronic, mechanical,
photocopying, recording, or otherwise, without the prior permission of the publisher.

D/2002/0095/79

ISBN 2-503-52203-3

THE FUTURE OF MEMORY

Edited by Giulio Blasi

Giulio Blasi	*Introduction*	7
Patrick Bazin	*Reconfigured memory*	21
Riccardo Ridi	*Digital heritage: Hardware, software and cultural policies in the library world*	35
Michele Santoro	*Libraries: Our future preserved*	45
Paolo Ciancarini e Michela Saviane	*The future of memory over the Internet*	63
Bruce Sterling	*The birth and death of memory*	83
Fabio Vitali	*On the duration of rich documents*	91
Andrea Babich	*Retrogaming: For a digital preservation of videogames*	115
Seamus Ross	*Digital preservation: Strategy, intervention, and accident*	137

Giulio Blasi

INTRODUCTION

**1. Temporal cycles of computer technologies:
The digital preservation problem**

One of the most pervasive effects of digital technologies is the fact that society tends to adapt itself to the temporal cycles and rhythms of the computer and software world.

The so called "Moore's Law" and the very nature of software, which is by definition a world of very mutable and evolving objects, make us accept as a matter of fact the rapid obsolescence cycles of digital technologies and their continuous substitution.

We usually associate such a rapid substitution pace to the marketing strategies of the big hardware and software corporations and we perceive (correctly of course) that the increase of software functions (e.g. the multimedia) is strictly complementary to the growth of speed and performance of hardware equipment.

In the last 10 years however a new interest has emerged regarding the possible effects of such substitution cycles on the conservation and preservation of digital materials. The report published in the US in 1996 by a *Task Force on Archiving of Digital Information*, created by the Research Library Group, is probably the most significant contribution to this first phase of the discussion.

Until the mid '90s, the problem of preserving digital materials had been posed only in terms of life expectancy of the memory supports of digital technologies: tape, floppy disks, etc. From this point of view, digital materials pose problems almost analogous to those relevant to the preservation of analogical materials such as audio and video on tape. A periodical refreshing of memory supports is the obvious and consolidated strategy to handle obsolescence problems or damage risks of these materials.

The report of the *Task Force on Archiving of Digital Information*, however, introduces a new field of problems regarding materials whose very codification structure has become obsolete. This of course is not necessarily specific of digital technologies, since a number of analogical communications technologies of the past have become obsolete. But with digital technologies the problem acquires a specific and astounding magnitude since there is a tradition of at least 40 years of creating enormous amounts of digital data collections of every conceivable nature.

Think for example of data processed with software applications and operating environments which are now obsolete. For example, records of a database stored on 960 bits punch cards for an old UNIVAC or IBM mainframe (the first exit poll in the history has been carried out for example with this technology in 1952, with the Eisenhower presidential campaign). In similar cases the data recovery poses problems definitively more complex and complicated than the simple refreshing of the physical memory support.

Without looking so far away in the past, let's recall some names of word processing systems publicised by Byte in the last 20 years : very obscure brands like PFS: write, Leading Edge, Samna, Multimate, Xwrite, DeScribe, Clearlook have parallel to names like Microsoft Word, Lotus Word Pro, Wordperfect.[1]

If we try to draw a matrix of all the possible dimensions of the problem (typologies of memory supports, hardware, operating systems, applications, programming languages, data formats and so on) it emerges very clearly that there will be no unemployment in the future in the sector of what we may call "digital archaeology".

To mention just the case of punch cards, we should consider enormous numbers: around 1967, only in the US, the average year production was of about 200 billions of punch cards, corresponding approximately to 400.000 tons of paper. Many Fortune 500 corporations (like Ford) and many sectors of the Public Administration still maintain today large data sets on punch cards to avoid the significant migration costs. Corporations like Cardamation Company (Phoenixville, Pennsylvania) occupy this quite unusual market niche.[2]

However the real problem is not the numbers dimension in itself but the fact that such a problem seems destined to re-emerge cyclically with an ever increasing magnitude. The exponential growth of the digital preservation problem is due to two main factors:

❑ every generation that finds some solution for preserving past digital materials transfer to future generations an equivalent problem that will emerge in a subsequent cycle;

INTRODUCTION 9

❑ on the basis of our present experience, it is quite likely that the quantity of digital objects that we'll have (potentially) to preserve from becoming obsolete will expand exponentially in the future. We'll have thus a cyclical re-emergence of an ever expanding problem.

Morris (from the University of Edinburgh) has noted that we can already try some historical periodisation of the digital preservation problem. He suggests a distinction mapped on the three fundamental periods in the history of Digital Information Technologies.

❑ the '50s, the period of the huge mainframes characterised by the creation of big data sets. Partly the work of digital preservation on these materials has been already done or it is beginning. It is very clear, however, that not everywhere in the world there are enough attention and resources to handle the problem. In the East European Countries, for example, a vast amount of these data sets are at risk of destruction and/or extinction;

❑ the late '70s and the '80s, with the PC revolution and the stabilisation of the four "classical" office applications: word processing, databases, spreadsheets and presentation. One of the specific problems of this period is the great variety of software and hardware platforms emerged in the first period of PC history, before the stabilisation of the "wintel" model in the '90s.

❑ the '90s, in which of course we are still radically immersed, dominated by Scott McNealy's mantra "The computer is the network": in this third period, digital conservation problems become even more complex as a consequence of the "distributed" nature of a large amount of data and applications. One of the prophets of our epoch of distributed hypermedia systems, Ted Nelson, has proposed a mental experiment for a radical reform of our literary system and its conversion into his distributed hypertext system called Xanadu. It is quite interesting that nowhere in his reflections we find a reference to time and to the problems related to the evolution of networking technologies and concepts. The Xanadu system was a sort of time-neutral theoretical construction. On the Internet, in contrast, such a problem is becoming crucial.

An interesting example of a sort of spontaneous initiative towards digital preservation comes from the videogames world. The virtual community of the so called "retrogamers" has developed a number of emulation programs that permit to play the ROM of old Arcade games appeared from the mid '70s on the modern PC. One of those communities, for example, has developed in Italy MAME (Multiple Arcade Machine Emulator), an application on which you can play over 1000 classic games appeared from 1975 up to the '80s. MAME is a freeware software and its co-operative development very much resembles the way the Linux operating system has emerged.

Emulation is another possible strategy for digital preservation together with refreshing and migration. According to Jeff Rothenberg, emulation is the only long-term strategy for digital preservation able "to recreate a digital document's original functionality, look, and feel" (Rothenberg 1998). This opinion is significantly close to the ideology of MAME developers:

> ...with MAME you can actually play over 1000 classic arcade video games on your PC. These are NOT recreations; these are the actual arcade games that appeared in arcades in the '70s and '80s. The game's code is dumped into ROM files that MAME loads and replays on your computer. The purpose of MAME is to actually pretend to be the CPU and support chips that these games need to play. MAME is the "hardware" of the arcade game, the ROMs are the "software". It was designed to digitally preserve games and gameplay that would otherwise be forgotten in the modern day rat race of console games and computers. <http://www.mame.net>

We will certainly hear in this conference about more "serious" case studies of digital rescue of obsolete materials. But I think the retrogamers example is very interesting because it opens on a small scale a number of crucial problems. First of all, copyright issues because it is not very clear what the license status of old software stuff is. Secondly, an identity problem. Not every digital preservation strategy is capable of preserving the identity (or a reasonable approximation) of the original object. The wide literature on this topic has proposed 5 fundamental strategies for digital preservation. I have already mentioned:

- *refreshing*, that is, the simple substitution of the physical memory support;
- *migration*, that is, some sort of re-cording of the object with up-to-date technologies;
- *emulation*, that is, software that allows to execute applications or read data formats on platform different from the one they were originally designed for.

All these strategies certainly pose specific problems and none of them is immune from the "identity problem". As Michael Lesk has noted, recent hypermedia systems with their typical mixture of programming languages and data types are very difficult to migrate (or emulate, I add) without deeply modifying the structure and code of the systems themselves.

We have thus the paradox that preserving digital objects inevitably leads to a mutation of the objects themselves. Historians like Roger Chartier have noted how the digitisation of paper materials could lead to a loss of meaning. This is certainly reasonable if you consider the paratextual apparatus and the physical dimension of the book as a meaningful element of the text.

> De là, pour notre présent, une forte leçon: le possible transfert du patrimoine écrit d'un support à un autre, du *codex* à l'écran, ouvre des possibilités immenses, mais il est aussi une violence faite aux textes, séparés des formes qui ont contribué à construire leur significations historiques. A supposer que, dans un avenir plus ou moins proche, les œuvres de notre tradition ne soient plus communiquées et déchiffrées que dans une représentation électronique, le risque serait grand de voir perdue l'intelligibilité d'une culture textuelle où un lien ancien, essentiel, à été noué entre le concept même de texte et une forme particulière du livre: le *codex*. (Chartier 1995: 38)

But what paratext is to text the graphic user interface is to software programs, and the paradox is that the risk envisaged by Chartier regarding the digitisation of our traditional libraries emerges now as a structural element of document preservation in the digital world.

To these three strategies of digital preservation we should add at least:

- *standardisation*, that is, investing in the backward compatibility and interoperability of data and applications;
- *conservation of hardware and software*, that is, creating ICT collections of old hardware devices and programs that one may re-use in the future to execute and read ancient programs and data.

Maybe we are less worried by these two strategies as regards identity (and copyright) of the original object. But unfortunately they pose other problems: an extensive process of standardisation is in fact unlikely, given the market reality of conflicting proprietary technologies, and museums and collections are not something that could be easily created and managed by the typical institutions that will collect large amounts of digital materials.

In the real world, perhaps, a mix of these 5 strategies is what most institutions and organisations involved in the digital preservation problem will experiment in the near future.

2. Internet and digital preservation: New dimension of the problem

One of the objectives of this conference is also to understand if these 5 strategies that have been articulated in the '90s are adequate to the new problems posed by the enormous diffusion of networking technologies, especially the Internet. Does the Internet pose new problems in this respect?

It is of course very difficult to answer this question but I think we can start looking at how the Internet is changing our idea of the Personal Computer and the idea of the computer in general. If we look specifically at the effects of World Wide Web technologies and standards we can distinguish 4 ways in which the web is changing the PC:

- applications embed web browsing functionalities (word processors are web editors and browsers, presentation tools like PowerPoint save in HTML formats like database and spreadsheets, etc.);
- web browsers and HTML pages embed applications (Java, JavaScript, VBScript, etc.);
- operating systems are shifting from the desktop to the browser metaphor (e.g. Windows 98);
- there are many attempts to export the browser model to simplified computing equipment (WebTV, Network Computer, etc.).

One of the consequences of these transformations is that the basic definitions of a hypertext (given by Ted Nelson and others) are now too simplified: hypertexts are not anymore non-sequential systems of text and multimedia objects. Hypertexts are today non-sequential systems of texts, multimedia components and applications. The notion of a *hypertext of applications* clearly poses new problems in terms of longevity of the web formats and standards.

In general, however, since the web model is propagating everywhere in the IT world, it is very likely that it will also affect our notion of digital memory. The three historical stages of the digital preservation problem I have mentioned before are in fact associated with three different "topologies" of the digital memory:

- a centralised model (typical of old mainframes but also, more recently, of many server based computing systems, network computing, applications servers);
- a decentralised model (typical of the Personal Computer culture, with software distribution based on a copy-per-license model);
- a distributed model (typical of Internet and the web, where documents are memorised across a number of different nodes on a network).

I can't resist the temptation to illustrate this distinction with a scheme from a very important paper published by Paul Baran (Rand Corporation) in 1964. This was probably one of the crucial seminal studies that led to the ARPANET/Internet project.

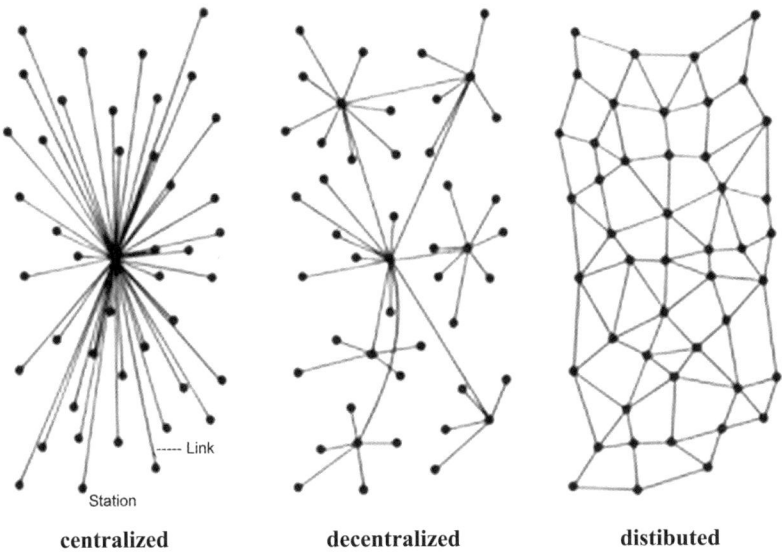

Figure 1. P. Baran "On Distributed Communication Networks" (RAND Corp. 1964).

The difficulties implied in the concept of "distributed memory" emerge quite clearly if one looks at the experiments that Brewster Kahle is conducting in the US with his *Internet Archive* initiative. Kahle's idea is simple and brilliant: he wants to make some sort of archive of the Internet and the World Wide Web. We know that somehow the first 30 years of the Internet history are like the *incunabula* of the early printing era. It would be a real pity if future generations could not accede to some sort of historical reference of how we are managing the emergence of this new element in our media configuration.

Kahle's idea is also feasible. The Internet Archive was started in 1996 and after one year they had already realised 3 snapshots of about 500.000 web sites amounting to 8TB of data. The scanning of the web is conducted every 30-60 days (see for more technical details at <http://www.archive.org>).

This very simple idea hides a number of problems. What does memorising a network of mutable interconnected documents and applications mean? In the lucky cases, it means taking a picture of a moving object. In the unlucky cases, it doesn't mean anything at all (for example you are not able to archive a database application, at list not by usual network spiders like Altavista and similar).

In particular, think of the hypertext link structure that characterises web documents. This structure is presumably the most dynamic and mutable on the web. From the point of view of digital preservation, links are the weakest elements of web documents. This means that snapshots of the web risk the loss of large areas of hypertext connectivity, which will imply some sort of archaeology and migration if this connectivity is to be recovered. It is thus evident that even the simplest operation of saving an HTML file poses short-term problems of re-usability. If you want a test of that, just try browsing "The '96 US Presidential Election Web Archive" realised by Kahle at www.archive.org. The archived sites are full of broken links and it is very clear that to re-use them would require some massive "archaeology" of the HTML code.

This is simply one example of the fact that this third phase of the ICT history is opening new and more complex problems in the area of digital preservation.

3. Social effects of the digital preservation problem

In this historical phase of the digital preservation problem, it is perhaps obvious and inevitable that we tend to focus on the practical and technological questions.

The problem of digital preservation, however, has effects on a number of social actors somehow involved in the process of accumulating digital collections. A very brief list of typical stakeholders includes:

- Libraries and Archives
- Electronic and Multimedia Publishers
- Public Administration
- Mass Media
- Corporations that need long term preservation of data from their information systems

In each of these sectors the problem of digital preservation will presumably assume specific shapes. A common element shared by all these subjects is the general economic model triggered off by the digital preservation problem. All the stakeholders will cyclically revisit their budget in order to take into account the new expenses related to the chosen strategy of digital preservation.

A systematic study of the economic impact of the digital preservation problem is still to be done but it is very clear that every organisation involved in the problem risks generating an exponential growth of costs and potential redundancies with other actors involved. This is why all the studies on this subject put great emphasis on co-operation among stakeholders.

A simple and practical example comes from the libraries that are today investing to transform themselves, somehow, into "digital" or "multimedia" libraries.

There is a very simple and general distinction with respect to what type of digital materials a library can hold. The digital preservation strategies and responsibilities of the libraries vary accordingly: a) materials originally digitised by the library itself; b) materials digitised and published by other subjects.

Intuitively, one should limit the preservation responsibility only to the first cases. In Bologna, for example, the Biblioteca dell'Archiginnasio has produced a digitised version of its historical XIX century catalogue. Of course, it will be the responsibility of this library to adopt adequate strategies to preserve this material in the future.

It seems also reasonable not to assign to libraries the burden of preserving materials of the second type. A long-term preservation strategy to preserve a catalogue of multimedia CD ROMs, for example, is the obvious responsibility of the publisher or at least of the copyright owner. Apart from questions about a very distant future in which neither the publisher nor the original copyright owner will exist anymore, several problems may emerge in this context even in the short term.

Indeed, suppose that a library has invested significant resources in the creation of a collection of CD ROMs, buying many licenses per title to allow concurrent accesses to the titles. Who will sustain the costs of the migration of the titles (or whatever other preservation strategy is adopted)?

We have here many different problems. First, it is very clear that multimedia publishers have a short term interest in upgrading their most requested titles to up-to-date technologies. These upgraded versions would be acquired by libraries that could thus dispose of titles adequate to HW and SW to date. This solution makes publishers responsible for digital preservation and leaves the library with the only task to keep their access infrastructures up to date (HW and basic SW).

This solution is of course valid only for the selected number of titles that (by market selection) publishers decide to migrate to non obsolete technologies. If we observe this process in the mid and long term, however, the situation will change dramatically because it is quite unlikely that publishers will invest serious resources in preserving titles only for a historical interest. As a consequence all the institutions with huge quantities of multimedia titles will remain alone in addressing the preservation problems raised by these materials.

Maybe this will oblige the libraries at least to co-operate with other preservation organisations if they want to keep the integrity of their multimedia collections in time. On the other hand, if they don't address the problem, there will be a periodic loss of part of their catalogues and a continuous substitution flow in the library possessions. As you understand immediately, a radical change of the accumulative model of accession of our traditional libraries toward a more fluid model of periodic substitution would not be without impact on the very concept of library emerged in the last two centuries and on our idea of historical memory.

Libraries, like all the other institutions involved in the digital preservation problem, have no definite strategies in the short and mid term.

4. Conclusions

There is a way to refer to McLuhan's analysis on the effects of communications technologies without falling into a simplistic technological determinism. Very often the emergence of new communications technologies determine problems and obstacles that oblige some areas of society to restructure their practices to cope with them.

This is quite reasonable if one thinks that when a new medium enters the system of media at a given time it leads, potentially at least, to a re-mapping of all the relationships within the traditional system of media. The computer and the networks like the Internet have been doing that for 30 years.

We usually associate new media to the new possibilities and practical advantages they seem to give. This is the typical *Wired* ideology of the "digerati". The digital preservation case, however, demonstrates that in parallel with the emergence of socially perceived advantages, new communications technologies impose constraints that are not (at least immediately) socially perceived but are nevertheless very important and effective in the way they could shape our use of the new medium.

The digital preservation problem is an evident example of constraints imposed on our traditional media system. In a recent article significantly titled "Why digitize?", Abby Smith has noted that "Much is gained by digitizing, but permanence and authenticity, at this juncture of technological development, are not among those gains" (Smith 1999). It is in fact a paradox that while we are here talking about the digital preservation problem, there are ongoing discussions and debates on digitisation as a preservation strategy of the old media!

The future of digital memory is certainly an open field of problems that quite unlikely we'll be able to reduce to the memorisation practices and models of our manuscript/typographic culture or to the XX century models of the mass broadcasting media: the problem of the identity of the digital objects in time, the copyright issues, the relationships between the stakeholders of the preservation process, the institutional roles of libraries and archives, the definition of new standards, the selection criteria of the digital materials to be preserved, the economic management and models of preservation strategies, and finally, the role of old media digitising initiatives. The reflection on digital preservation opens these and many other problems. I hope that this conference will help us exchange ideas on some of them.

I think our awareness of the problem is growing in this period in coincidence with the first example that will focus our attention and interests on a planetary scale. I am referring of course to the so called "Y2K Bug", which is, at least indirectly, a digital preservation problem: apart from electrical plants, airports and financial institutions, the risk (particularly serious in the Eastern world) also involves the integrity of data and information based today on 2 digits processing.

The digital preservation problem appears thus less dramatic and urgent. It has a subtler way of introducing itself: someone tries to accede to some digital document, one day, and realises that there is no way to recover all or part of it.

Maybe only historians perceive this as a nightmare. I don't know if this is a nightmare or not, but I am sure we are facing an important and structural issue of our new media system. At least from this perspective, I hope this conference will help extend the perception of the problem.

Notes

[1] See Lesk <http://www.lesk.com/mlesk/auspres/aus.html>.

[2] See Wired 7.03: 142.

References and on line resources

BEAGRIE, N. & D. GREENSTEIN
1998 "A Strategic Policy Framework for Creating and Preserving Digital Collections", <http://www.ukoln.ac.uk/services/elib/papers/supporting/pdf/framework.pdf>

BENNETT, J.C.
1997 "A framework od data types and formats, and issues affecting the long term preservation of digital material", JSC/NPO Studies, British Library Research and Innovation Centre.

BLASI, G.
1999 *Internet. Storia e futuro di un nuovo medium*, Milano: Guerini e Associati.

BLASI, G. & A. BERNARDELLI (EDS.)
1995 "Introduction. Semiotics and the effects of media change research programmes. An overview of methodology and basic concepts", *VS*, 72: 3-28.

CHARTIER, R.
1995 "Le message écrit et ses réceptions. Du *codex* à l'écran", *VS*, 72: 29-42.

DAY, M. & N. BEAGRIE
1998 *DELOS6: Presevration of Digital Information*, <http://www.ariadne.ac.uk/issue16/delos>

GALLUZZI, P. & P.A VALENTINO (EDS.)
1996 *I formati della memoria*, Firenze: Giunti.

GRAUBARD, S.R. & P. LECLERC (EDS.)
1998 *Books, Bricks and Bytes. Libraries in the Twenty-first Century*, London: Transaction Publishers.

INTRODUCTION   19

GREGORY, T. & M. MORELLI
1994 *L'eclisse delle memorie*, Bari: Laterza.

HIGGS, E. (ED.)
1998 *History and Electronic Artefacts*, Oxford: Clarendon Press.

KAHLE, B.
1997 "Archiving the Internet", *Scientific American* (March).

LESK, M.
    Preserving Digital Objects: Recurrent Needs and Challenges,
    <http://www.lesk.com/mlesk/auspres/aus.html>

LIBRARY OF CONGRESS
    Digital Library Resources,
    <http://lcweb.loc.gov/loc/ndlf/digital.html>

LYMAN, P. & P. KAHLE
1998 "Archiving Digital Cultural Artifacts. Organising an Agenda for Action", D-Lib,
    <http://www.dlib.org/sdlib/july98/07lyman.html>

MAME
    <http://www.mame.net>

ROTHENBERG, J.
1998 *Avoiding Technological Quicksand: Finding a Viable Technical Foundation for Digital Preservation*,
    <http://www.clir.org/pubs/reports/rothenberg/contents.html>

SMITH, A.
1999 *Why Digitize?*
    <http://www.clir.org/pubs/reports/pub80-smith/pub80.html>

STERLING, B.
1994 *Heawy Weather* (trad.it. *Atmosfera mortale*, Milano: Bompiani: 1995)

STERLING, B. (ET AL.)
    Dead Media Project,
    <http://www.deadmedia.org>

TASK FORCE ON ARCHIVING DIGITAL INFORMATION
1996 *Preserving Digital Documents*,
    <http://www.rlg.org/ArchTF/tfadi.index.htm>

Patrick Bazin

RECONFIGURED MEMORY

Updating: this is indeed the daily ritual of any numerical activity. There will be no more of those erasures and slips of paper a writer used to leave to posterity for the great delight of textual genetics. No more scaffolding to trace first drafts, no more superimposition of changes accumulating on a painter's canvas, behind the final image, which could be handed over to the multiple deciphering of cultural archæology. The digital work (literary, artistic, etc.), cut off from the concrete conditions of its gestation, with neither traces nor history, appears in its rigid operating functionality.

In other words, the numerical activity might seem to produce oblivion as fast as it allows texts and cultural objects to proliferate in huge numbers and swamp their networks. Its memorizing capacity, whatever its exponential growth, would, in fact, serve an eternal present, devoid of depth. What it would gain in extension and diversity, as its empire spreads rapidly to all the domains of human activity, would be linked to a corresponding loss in retrospective depth, and especially, by eradicating its roots within a material genealogy, in authenticity. It would be in contradiction with all notions of cultural heritage – which would appear to need a monumentality, or, at the very least, traces of this monumentality.

How paradoxical! Just as we are witnessing an unprecedented reinforcement of humanity's memory capacity, the threat of amnesia brought on by dematerialization of the mediums and speed of inscription, destroying as fast as they create, would seem to weigh on our cultural future. Especially in France, this fear generates a vast discourse in defence of slowness, which bases itself on the resistance of the inscription material, on the progressive sedimentation of archives, and on the necessary capillarity of cultural transmission. According to this pessimistic vision, well illustrated in the latest issue of the French magazine *Le Débat* (1999), where George Steiner, among others, wonders whether the humanities are not reaching their twilight, cultural memory implies, by definition, a slow and repetitive impregnation – the scholarly reading of the fundamental texts being a good model of this.

1. Book and memory

This point of view is indeed based on the book/reading pair, whose memorizing power plays, as it were, with the articulation between fixity and mobility: on the one hand, a thought content, inscribed permanently in a stable medium, while also being easy to carry and spread through printed reproductions; on the other hand, the individual act of reading, volatile and creative, whose interpretative freedom can only express itself fully in a confrontation with the resistance of the page, which slows it down. Like an initiatory process, each reading of a single book slowly traces the path which so many others have followed, and reproduces the miracle of an act which is singular as well as collective, since it is shared by the community of readers. This is how a network of multiple interpretations is woven around literary and art works, interpretations which, while starting from the same books, produce new texts and, by doing so, perpetuate the living memory of book culture. This culture thus involves a scattering and transmission apparatus that, contrary to oral tradition, has the great advantage of encouraging an interpretative diversification, building nevertheless a coherent and cumulative memory. And it is precisely this coherent accumulation of diversity, based on the great stability of the medium, which, for some people, would appear to be threatened by numerical archives.

Although I am a librarian and a book lover, I will try to show that, whatever the risks inherent in any innovation, this fear is basically groundless. Far from being opposed to the established order of books, or to other traditional means of conservation, numerical technology carries the hope that it will considerably improve the answer they have provided up to now to the old problem of cultural memory. Not only will this improvement lead to a mechanical increase in the retrospective depth and the size of the memory, but, especially – and this is paramount – it will enhance its power to evoke, and thus gain in complexity and richness.

In reality, the faulty assessment which leads some people to criticize the impact of numerical archives within the cultural domain is often due to a confusion between the well-tried solution and the problem itself, for instance, being unwilling to admit that a tool such as the book is not an end in itself, but simply a means to resolve a more fundamental problem, i.e., the development of ideas and their circulation among men. Thus, the book is too often likened to the text and it is thought that if the former is under threat, the latter is also threatened. One is then led to use the book as a criterion to evaluate an electronic text, instead of wondering whether the latter could not represent an improved form of textuality, freed from the prison and linearity of the book.

It is obvious that, in the present state of technology, the book in its paper form benefits from ergonomic assets and from an emotional aura which do not apply to the screen. It is also obvious that the, through an intensive mode of reading that tries to squeeze the maximum of meaning from each text, civilisation of the book has favoured an analytical way of thinking whose success does not need any demonstration, and which is today jeopardized by the browsing possibilities opened up by numerical textuality. However, instead of lamenting the relative depreciation that has affected the intellectual mode of life which, up to now, has surrounded the book form of the text, it would be better to analyze the mutation of textuality itself, as well as the new path it has opened up with hypertext links, interactivity and networking.

The same applies to memory. If it were to be likened to storage too much – either in a library or in a museum –, access to intangible data being the only issue, there would be a risk of not grasping the problem in its entirety; this problem being one of transmission of cultural life, or rather, of transmission as an intrinsic element of cultural life.

Among the means to simplify the problem, two in particular are of particular concern to the archiving specialist: the permanence of the mediums and the durability of coding and reading programs. These preoccupations are indeed legitimate, and call for appropriate measures, but we will see that they do not bear on what is essential. Let us analyze them.

2. The false question of the medium

The first of these preoccupations, that of the inscribing mediums, mainly affects the digital disks used to store texts, images and sounds, for they are not expected to last more than a few decades. And in fact, as far as the text is concerned, microfilms still are, at the moment, the stablest medium, since they have a life expectancy of at least a century. Thus, if one wants to evaluate archiving efficacy in terms of medium resistance over time, microfilms remain the safest and cheapest way to preserve, for instance, the content of nineteenth-century newspapers, whose acid paper destroys itself from day to day. On the other hand, it goes without saying that numerical mediums allow access to the content with an ease and comfort so much greater than what can be done with microfilm. They provide, for example, direct and instantaneous means of access to a specific part of a text lost in the middle of a vast corpus, as well as remote access. Moreover, the increasing speed of copying onto a numerical medium, to which should be added the reduction in cost of various forms of mass storage, leads us to think that huge quantities of data will become easy to save, and even that these archives will be duplicated. Finally, despite the relative precariousness of the medium, digital storage appears more and more to be the solution of the future. It should be added that, in a number of countries, the most precious archives, such as the registry office, are increasingly stored in digital form. Thus, in the space of a few years, the problem of the medium to be used appears to have definitely been solved.

The reason for this turning point is linked to the fact that conservation of content does not now depend on the durability of the medium, and to the fact that the conservation techniques of the digitalized heritage will no longer concentrate on protection of or restoring the mediums, as was the case up to now, but on migration of content. One might even be right in thinking that current research being carried out in certain heritage institutions in order to manufacture absolutely permanent numerical disks – made of glass or gold – is completely anachronistic.

Furthermore, there is nothing new in making a distinction between medium and content, since, without this distinction, memorization would have been impossible and the problem of memory would not have existed. For example, the text transmitted by copyists in the Middle Ages has to be differentiated from the various codices on which it was inscribed, and the printed text from the physical copies used to scatter it. It is precisely the relative independence of the information in relation to its medium which characterizes the fact that an event – e.g., a thought – has become a memory object that can be recalled, and not simply something that manifests itself or persists in its being. Does not the historical monument itself acquire its memorial efficacy when, having lost its original function, it has become a document and a reading object? The whole history of memorization techniques coincides with the progressive separation of memory contents from their mediums.

Thus, while there are as many versions, more or less corrupt, of a manuscript text as there are codices containing this text, the printed text generally remains the same from one copy to the next, at least for the same edition. The advent of numerical archives has thus only radicalized a process of increasing abstraction which, while improving memorization, detaches the memory object from its iconic aspect, and gradually depreciates the cult which used to surround it. This shows that the false question concerning the durability of numerical mediums is linked to the fear of a loss of aura and not to a real concern about efficacy.

3. The obsolescence of languages

A second, much more serious preoccupation stems from the rapid obsolescence of the programs which encode the data to be stored and make it accessible. Indeed, what would become of the numerical image of an illumination, without the format encoding it, without the operating system which allows it to appear on the screen? Once digitalized, this image becomes an algorismic construct whose consistency depends on the correct sequence of reasoning and on the grammatical chain it is made of. This is to say that a numerical image, like any numerical object, depends entirely on the rules of the language in which it is implemented and on the correct application of these rules. It is thus entirely made up of language. Its conservation and accessibility depend directly on the capacity of this language to be understood or translated. What then would be the use of a numerical image left in a state of potentiality when the language describing it can no longer be interpreted by a computer system, or, when the image is in a marginal and untranslatable proprietary format? This situation is made even more complicated because the memory object, if it is to be efficient in its numerical form, should have the ability to manifest itself in extremely varied contexts, belonging to diverse uses (for example, on different types of screens or at very different calculating speeds). It should not depend on one program only, but on an operating environment implying the co-operation of an increasing number of operators.

To the fairly simple problem of migration from one medium to another has thus been added a much more delicate problem, that of the evolution and interoperability of computer languages, in a context of permanent "linguistic" innovation and competition. The numerical form of cultural memory now depends on an accelerating technical evolution, as well as on an expanding knowledge economy. Up to now, technical progress improved continuously the conservation and appropriation processes of cultural memory (we only have to think of such diverse innovations as writing, printing, photography, libraries and their catalogues, the de-acidifying of paper, microfilms, etc.). Today, it would seem that, as soon as progress is made, it becomes obsolete. Here again, there are two ways to react to this difficulty.

4. The fear of an eternal present

The first one consists of doubting that it is possible to preserve, in the long term, any cultural memory worthy of the name. This argument is thus not really technical, but rather, socio-economical and philosophical. It springs from the principle that, given the complexity and cost of successive migrations, saving memory will be confronted with mutually opposed interests, and the only things left will be those elements which have been able to adapt to the practical needs of the moment. Worse, what will survive will bear no relation to the original, since it will have been entirely restructured: attached to a hyperlink network, the original text as such will have ceased to exist; the digitalized image will have been enhanced or distorted; an interactive 3-D virtual literary or art work will have lived a number of different lives.

While recognizing that cultural memory has always been the result of a selection, and that this memory is perpetually being reconstructed, this argument is based on the fact that the rules of the game change when the memory object is no longer an object retaining, despite transformations, a link with the original, but is the transient result of calculations. This memory postulates that, up to now, reconstruction of the cultural memory was based on traces that had the value of evidence. Even when a document was forgotten in the depths of a museum, or when an item of future heritage was destroyed, there remained, as it were, a negative shape, the trace of the event. Things have changed with numerical archives, which, despite an unprecedented storage capacity, operate an active act of oblivion as they ceaselessly reconfigure memory from within. Basically, this criticism bears on the nature of the act of oblivion: it argues that it would be better to be faced with a real oblivion, which emphasizes what deserves to survive and endows it with its true cultural value, rather than with an eternal present where every cow is grey.

The second approach, which is mine, accepts all the preceding remarks, but the conclusions it draws from them are diametrically opposed. As is often the case with such debates concerning the impact of new technologies on culture, the differences do not concern so much an analysis of the techniques themselves, their advantages and disadvantages, as the idea one has of their field of application, in this case the function of memory. Either it is thought that the question of cultural memory, as it has appeared up to now in the context of historically-determined technologies and societies, constitutes an impassable horizon – the yardstick to be used in order to contemplate the future; or one shifts one's gaze to see whether the nature of the problem is not evolving.

Indeed, what could be said of an approach that would assess printing only from the point of view of an oral culture, criticising it for not leaving enough space for the biological memory? Could one not imagine, on the contrary, that whatever, in the numerical field, appears most to contradict the usual conservation criteria, is in fact a renewed chance for cultural memory, i.e., a permanent capacity to re-create and an accrued sensitivity to the socio-economical environment?

5. The creative memory

This capacity for re-creation can be explained first by the strong potential for linking data, but also by the fact that the numerical memory often implements, in addition to objects, production processes for objects; to a certain extent, it is as if books implemented their own publication and distribution processes. This is already partly true of the heritage now being digitalized a posteriori, but much more true of the cultural heritage of the future, which will consist of an increasing volume of native numerical data, such as hypertexts, electronic libraries, newsgroups, discussion forums, clusters of internet sites whose links will be stored, etc.

De facto, a heritage object with no link to a specific context can have no memorial value. The work of memory is precisely that of re-establishing links which would give meaning to this object by tying it to its synchronic environment, and to its line of ascendancy. This applies to the philological analysis of a text as well as to the comparison between various types of Greek pottery. This specifically documentary work is complemented by a simulation effort – some would speak more simply of imagination – aiming at reconstituting the object's functional space and at understanding its potentialities. For example, it will be easier to understand chipped flint if one personally does the chipping, and uses the flint to cure a skin.

Memory, seen as a continent, thus presents itself as a space for exploration and experimentation, exactly as in present reality. Obviously, memory is not simply the re-use of a past which would speak for itself, in the same way that knowledge is not the immediate grasp of a clear and distinct reality which comes in contact with the mirror of conscience. The memory object, like the object of knowledge in the present, has nothing to say and could even be said not to exist as long as it has not been made to speak. It only exists through the network of links woven around it through a mixture of culture and cognitive engineering. It only exists as a function of present-day preoccupations and tools. It is an intrinsic component of the present. Thus, what improves the memory is not, as such, the number of archived objects, or even, of course, the archiving systems (a library with no readers is a dead letter); on the contrary, it is the development of data-processing systems which not only gives meaning to heritage, but also helps it grow.

The general "patrimonalisation" which we are experiencing today has no other explanation: the increasing capability to treat all reality as a data web, or as a document, ends up by transforming every thing, every event, as both an echo from the past and the material for a future exploration. There is nothing backward-looking or reactionary in this evolution; rather, the manifestation of a desire to know, that is, no longer satisfied with a phantasmal, self-sufficient and brutal present which would be opposed to the soft nostalgia of the "mal d'archive" so dear to scholars. The heritage aspect, which today colours most scientific and educational approaches, including the study of the background noise of the universe, takes in what is real as a continuum, and memory as an implementation of the future.

6. The electronic library

Thus, one might say that numerical archiving has come just in time, since it exteriorizes and instrumentalizes the memory capacities of man, with a power heretofore unknown by the archiving and data-processing techniques.

Let us simply take the example of the shift from traditional libraries to electronic libraries. As a retention locus, the former was also an enclosed representation space where the internal logic of books – those capsules of stabilized text – was also increased by a strict mediative apparatus meant to guide the reader. It worked as a settling tank where, through use of a succession of filters, fairly independent of content and designed a priori (catalogue structure, shelving classification, layout of the rooms), sedimented, hierarchic knowledge was organized. One could always plunge into its depth and retrieve exotic messages, but the quest for singularity always had to operate within the framework of a common topology, of an integrative encyclopædia.

The space of the electronic library is very different. There are no walls; it is wide open to the exponential diversity of data sources which are accessible through networks. But it also unfurls dynamically around the relationships, from text to text, from term to term, having arisen during reading or during the creation of a corpus, and these, in turn, produce an operating meta-text. The D-Lite program at Stanford University Library is a good example of this mode of operation, where a meta-corpus in constant evolution is built up from scientific articles and hypertext links.

The electronic library is thus permanently restructured through its own operating mode. Its ability to interconnect diverse objects increases as it functions, and it applies to historical data as well as to present events, integrating them into an ever wider set. It thus is much more capable than the traditional library of linking heterogeneous viewpoints and traditions, of rapidly changing its perspective, of relativizing cultural barrier, and of disturbing academic procedures. Its specific development axis is no longer that of horizontal classification or diachronic accumulation, but that of increasing complexification, which is precisely, to my mind, the main vector of an active memory.

However, the example of electronic documentation, as it is practised today, is fairly limited. The development of intelligent agents capable, for instance, of tracing the semantic cartography of a vast set of texts, or of making use of research paths to re-inject their logic into new contexts, will decisively improve the management of documentary complexity. They will not so much enable the user to automatize certain research as to help men in developing decontextualization strategies, so that they do not remain caught by stereotypes.

Indeed, in many respects, the use of cultural memory has remained very conservative up until now, even if it has freed itself from the redundancy of orality. Historical schools and hermeneutic traditions plough their own furrows without ever really coming into contact. They even have a tendency to transform their inertia into an asset. Thus, building up scientifically-valid knowledge would appear to necessarily imply the epistemological enclosure of its field and the self-reproduction of a body of specialists with well-defined frontiers. In reality, one may wonder whether this set-up of procedures is not the counterpart of an anthropological limit which would hinder individuals in such a way as to stop them from playing different pieces of music at the same time. From then on, the arrival of authentic knowledge engineering is more than likely to change the set-up by exteriorizing the various types of cognitive behaviour and by increasing their number. As I said earlier, the future of memory is certainly no longer linked to the retention and inscription modes, but to the improvement of processing systems.

7. Simulation and event

Among these, as we have seen, simulation has long held a privileged position, since it enables the reconstitution of objects or facts from the traces they have left, and the opening up of their potential, as was the case with chipped flint. As it happens, a simulation capacity is consubstantial with the computing nature of numerical data. It takes on a speed and a flexibility which it reaches neither with concrete experimentation nor even with mental experience, to such an extent that numerical calculation can produce literally unthinkable mathematical objects, which can only be translated through figuration with computer-generated images.

It can, a fortiori, generate objects or situations very close to our common experience, and which will come to inhabit our world more and more, be it in industry, medicine or creative arts. Few sections of the real world will not profit from building models this way, at one time or another, from the conception stage up to the memory stage. These models will, no doubt, invest the numerical library of tomorrow, where they will be present both as memory objects, with all their characteristic flexibility and re-creation ability, and as tools for documentary research, or rather, as what we will have to see as documentary experimentation. There is, of course, no question of mistaking them for concrete experience, of which they are only a simulacrum. No more, indeed, than a novel such as *Remenbrance of Things Past* can be mistaken for the vast open spaces of life. However, in both cases, it is the operating power of the procedure that matters, its capability to evoke, explore, remember, recreate. In fact, the act of simulation is an essential component of memory; this is why the contribution to memory by numerical data is so important in what we are talking about today.

Nevertheless, the future of memory does not lie only in the evolution of its tools. It also depends on the cultural reality which will be available tomorrow. And it is obvious that numerical data, picking up, by the way, where film and television left off, is in the process of appreciably modifying the terms of the cultural stakes. I will take an example that is dear to me, the written work.

Can one still think that the book form of a text will remain the only one at a time when a textuality without borders, mobile and forceful, invades the Internet? This way of writing and reading is only, like the book, one way of producing ideas by sharing them and enabling them to circulate widely; but, and this is where it differs from the book, it is difficult to store and sanctuarize. With the Internet, textuality has lost a good deal of the hieratic attributes that have made of the book, more than a document, a monument: enclosure, stability, juridical legitimacy and depth. It aims to produce an immediate effect on a community of quasi-interlocutors. In a certain way, it becomes performative, favouring short texts, zapping, fast reactions. It develops collectively, without final a author and without a final literary or art work, just as one holds a conversation. Seen from Sirius, it probably looks more like an ecosystem than like a library full of active readers.

In any event, does this mean that it will not be part of tomorrow's cultural memory and that, more generally, the events produced every second on the Net will not participate in it? It would naturally be rash to pretend that we are aiming at a culture without definite literary or art works and without authors, a culture made up of interventions and actors, but we may, without taking too many risks, prepare ourselves to enlarge the field of our memory to take in a much more composite and shifting memory than the one the museums and libraries have accustomed us to.

8. Memory, stake for society

The challenges confronting us, because of the reactivity of numerical tools, appear to be opposed to everything that seemed, up to now, to be the essence of a collectively-organized memory. Unless it is, on the contrary, as I have mentioned a few times, the sign of an unprecedented mobilization of the social community around its memory.

One obvious example of this evolution recently struck me, when we were given the task, in France, to undertake a vast computerization of rare book collections, centred on the Bibliothèque nationale. I was extremely surprised to see that, within a few years, not only millions of entries had been processed, but that a vast cataloguing activity, and even, at times, the numerization of long-forgotten collections had been undertaken, and that the hidden treasures of our written memory had started to appear on the Internet, for the great pleasure of the international scientific community. In reality, what generations of scholars had not wanted or been able to do, since they had too often been confined to something which had been given the pompous name of "Benedictine work", achieved in a trice by today's machines, had been given the status of a national cause, sustained by the combined efforts of technology, the authorities, and a generation of young librarians, enthusiastic about the Internet. This small parable attempts to show, once more, that the desire to spread and communicate is not automatically an enemy of memory, and that discourses which link memory to retention, under the guise of defending the humanities, can sometimes lead to opposite results.

In reality, as was shown by Manuel Castells in his work on the *Rise of the Network Society* (Oxford, Blackwell: 1996), we are changing into a society where knowledge will no longer be a tool of the economy, but its object itself, where knowledge engineering will be the main motor, from the film and television industry to biotechnology. Can one then seriously imagine that memory, that fundamental dimension of knowledge, could be excluded from the game, under the pretext that its most sacred, but also its most rigid forms, are challenged by less mumbling tools?

On the contrary, collective mastery of memory becomes a major asset, as is proved by the unprecedented international efforts to develop technologies, formats and norms capable, for example, of identifying sources (Digital Object Identify), of describing precisely the content of documents (metadata), of marking data, of endowing heuristic paths with a readability, etc. All these attempts possess the essential characteristic of aiming, from the start, at the widest opening and interoperability. They prove that mastering memory can only, from now on, be achieved through an exchange economy. This is certainly not a new relationship: the book, capsule of memory, is an operator of intellectual exchange. However, what is new is, as it were, the implementation, at the collective stage, of an individual cognitive phenomenon, i.e., the close entanglement between the constitution of the memory and innovation; the permanent reconfiguration of memory in contact with action.

Nevertheless, there will be obstacles on the path of the emergence of a more active cultural memory, the most difficult one will not be nostalgia, but the tribalization of public space. Of course, the new knowledge networks will soon be laying the foundations of more reactive knowledge, better able to integrate a large diversity of experience, and more equally shared. But these efforts will only prevent the identity fragmentation threatening any management of complexity if national and international bodies look into it. The stakes are political. They have to do with the collective capacity to maintain an authentic public space of knowledge, and thus to build up a common memory. As concerns this, the traditional role played by mediative institutions, such as, for example, public libraries, will remain of utmost importance. It may be that the great tutelary figures of memory, of which the book is one, are gradually leaving the stage, but the continued need of a cultural future for humanity implies obviously that their ancient teaching be saved.

Riccardo Ridi[1]

DIGITAL HERITAGE: HARDWARE, SOFTWARE AND CULTURAL POLICIES IN THE LIBRARY WORLD[2]

Nowadays it is not fashionable to speak of the bibliographical "patrimony" and of its conservation – to the extent that accusing someone of upholding a "patrimonial conception" of libraries or culture has become a serious offense. This is the reason why I prefer to speak of "heritage", a term perhaps a little less compromised by the economic and inventory-related aspects of preservation. Nevertheless, this short talk will deal with conservation and transmission to future generations.[3]

In libraries one does not deal with the conservation of single unique objects, as in museums, or of single original documents, as in historic archives. With the advent of the Gutenberghian "technical reproducibility" of documents, the task of those libraries known (pointedly) as "conservational" becomes the preservation of a single exemplar of a printing of identical copies as a guarantee of the "publication" of that impression in its entirety.[4]

But what does "being published" mean? Before the invention of printing it meant being read in public, or transcribed in a handful of exemplars all irremediably different from one another.[5] After the invention of the Web it means relying on a server which is telematically connected to all the computers in the world. Only the so-called "legislator" – this dusty scribe who jots down laws and public competitions in a cubicle isolated from the world – continues to think that being published is something indissolubly connected with creaking presses, printers dishing out tomes and prefectures receiving obligatory exemplars – crystallising characteristics which belong only to the Gutenberghian phase of editorial production. The concept of "being rendered public" in relation to a document has remained unchanged over the centuries, although technologies and methods have changed significantly, as can be noted by all those who, in the mean time, have nothermetically covered their eyes and stopped their ears.

There is much talk about the revolution caused in the universe of documents (Nelson's famous docuverse) by the advent of the electronic publishing industry. However, from the point of view of the evolution of the concept of "publication", the CD-Rom is terribly similar to the book, because it maintains unaltered the concepts of edition (discrete variant of a work) and exemplar (in an 'impression' of more or less identical copies), and because, in the library, it can be acquired, inventoried, catalogued, stored, lent, lost and expelled, just like a book.

Since they continue to deal with portable electronic supports, libraries remain within the furrow of tradition, and partially overlap with a "cousin" institution that in certain environments is seen as the very embodiment of the "patrimonial conception" of culture: the museum. The museum deals with unique exemplars; the library with archetypal exemplars. But in each case they are exemplars, that is, physical objects (made of atoms, as Negroponte would say). The real conceptual leap is only to be had with network publishing, electronic publishing on the net, Internet and the consequent radical reorganisation and transformation of the ever "local" classic documentary chain into an authentic hypertextual documentary network, which, for the most part, is "remote".[6]

Let us consider, for example, the theme of the obsolescence of the software and hardware instruments necessary for the reading of electronic documents – above all for the reading of multimedia documents, which are more sophisticated and thus more critical than a banal, though stabler text, in ASCII.[7] The problem is well known: the physical lifetime of digital multimedia supports (electronic, magnetic or optic) is not known with certainty, and may well be inferior to that of clay, stone, papyrus, parchment and paper.

However, if the issue was merely the physical lifetime of the supports, it would "suffice" to remove their contents from one support to another, and the inevitable "forgetfulness" that certain generations show for certain documents would become the inevitable documentary "cultural selection" that every generation makes before passing on those texts to successive generations.[8] This solution could even solve the problem of increasingly rapid obsolescence – which I am not sure whether to define "technological" or "commercial" – of the typology of the supports (and of devices able to decipher them) available on the market.

A much bigger problem, which risks involving *all* digital documents, independently of the value that academia and society at large can accord them, is that of the survival of a software that can translate digital data – written in a thousand different languages – into information assimilable by human input devices (eyes and ears) and hardware devices able to hold such programmes.[9]

The mere conservation of a CD-Rom is useless, if a suitable hardware reader does not survive alongside it; but even if data are periodically transferred into supports for the future, the survival both of programmes able to comprehend such data and translate them into a humanly comprehensible language, and of computers on which those programmes are run, remains problematic. Apart from the huge problem of the temporal transmission of linguistic messages of any nature and on any support (which is, for example, subject to the risk that, in the mean time, the memory of the language in which they were codified has been lost), electronic documents must confront at least four further specific risks which threaten their survival in time:

1. Brief physical duration of the supports for the memorisation of data (cd-rom, floppy disks, tapes, etc.).

2. Obsolescence of the hardware for the deciphering of the supports (readers, drives, etc.).

3. Obsolescence of the software for the interpretation of data (word processors, graphics programs, browsers, Acrobat reader etc.).

4. Obsolescence of the hardware for the execution of interpretation programs (microprocessors, computers, etc.)

There are two principal strategies for confronting these problems concerning the conservation of digital documents: "the first consists in translating them into standard formats independent of any computer system; the second in maintaining the legibility of the documents by extending the longevity of the computer system and their original software. Unfortunately both methods involve grave inconveniences."[10]

The first solution is a little too similar, in my opinion, to other grand utopias – such as universal language or automatic translation – to be considered realistic.[11] The second, though upheld by authoritative scholars of librarianship,[12] who relate this new function of computer archaeology to the more classical function of library philology,[13] risks being similarly unrealistic, at least in Italy, where the libraries, as regards technology and other aspects are shamefully backward. For example, it is difficult to imagine that the two Italian central national libraries, which are already under stress as a result of the management of paper material from the legal deposit, could also manage to act as library-museums in which extinct hardware and software products might be preserved and kept in use.[14]

A radical change in perspective occurs when one shifts from the *ownership* of portable supports, such as floppy disks and CD-Roms, to the remote *access* to electronic documents available, more or less for free, in the Internet. In the networked environment the construction of museums of computer archaeology loses the priority, while the Universal Bibliographical Control (UBC) – at least of the principal versions of documents which are incessantly updated on the net, often rapidly migrating from one server to another – becomes a current practice again.

Servers and addresses change, so do clients and browsers, but files corresponding to documents can preserve a great stability on the net, at least from the point of view of the legibility of the format – above all if one, in order to perfect graphic performance, has had the sagaciousness not to change standards originally oriented only to the logic structure of documents such as HTML, XML and SGML.[15] A standard HTML file, free from owners tags and stratagems for "freezing" a given graphic visualisation, is legible on browsers of all brands and on all operative systems, independently of the type of support on which it is held or copied.[16]

But future historians and ordinary readers will get little consolation from being able to read without difficulty the antique web pages handed down to them by previous generations if the quantitative consistency of the pages is too exiguous. If no one assumes the responsibility of "archiving Internet" – that is, of preserving and indexing the principal variants of the documents available on the net that succeed one another in time – the World Wide Web will be for ever doomed to live in an eternal "present" of updated documents, devoid of a historic dimension. Moreover, even leaving aside "editions" and "variants" of still available documents, there are web pages which, after being in the Internet for some time, suddenly disappear without leaving any trace.

On the one hand, there is the illusion of systematic self-musealisation of some utopian projects[17] addressing, with a lot of enthusiasm and a bit of superficiality, the huge problem of storing, preserving, accessing and cataloguing of an enormous, ever-changing hypertext like the Web. On the other hand, there is the fatalism of those who think, and they are partly right, that the really important documents will always survive thanks to updatings, re-editions, citations, local copies and transferrals to other media. However, a third path can be also beaten. This consists of the possible attempt to preserve for posterity at least those electronic documents in the Internet (not only web pages but also mailing list archives, newsgroups, gophers etc.) that are considered as the stablest, the most finished, identifiable and describable. The same thing occurs in more traditional fields in most countries of the world, when one attempts to obtain the Universal Bibliographic Control (UBC) and the Universal Availability of Publications (UAP)[18] through the agencies of national libraries and the legal deposit, which cover a vast percentage of, though not all the documents produced.

The first solution that can be proposed is that those subjects that receive the legal paper deposit should also manage the electronic deposit. Notwithstanding the banality of the idea, it would not seem to be particularly widespread;[19] but perhaps one could devise something better.

In the past I have maintained that a library can legitimately insert into its catalogue only those electronic periodicals that are locally preserved in its electronic shelves.[20] I will indulge, for a moment, in self-criticism. This approach is almost always too onerous for a single library. Must we therefore resign ourselves to having faith, for future access to the issues, in the continuity of our subscriptions for the current year and in publishers' inscrutable archiving policies? Not at all: the solution should rather consist of the co-operation between libraries in the creation of centralised and shared serials libraries.[21]

This approach could be also extended to include non-periodical electronic documents and thus lead to positive results – as long as we can learn from the errors of the Italian SBN (Servizio Bibliotecario Nazionale) as well as other unfinished gigantic national projects, and turn, rather, to groups of more restricted and homogenous co-operating libraries (according to geographic, disciplinary or typological vicinity, etc.). Thus, with a proper co-ordination and the identification of a subset of pertinent documents, a distributed national digital library could emerge.[22] Such an entity would guarantee indexing, remote access and storage to prevent authorial or editorial changes of mind. It could also conduct experiments in the field of PURL.[23]

To summarise, there are seven counteractions to the specific risks run by electronic documents due to the dangers of the passing of time:

1. Periodical transferral onto current digital supports.

2. Periodical translation into current languages and software.

3. Adoption of standard language and software.

4. Creation of software libraries, hardware museums and libraries of software emulators of hardware.

5. Preference for distribution on the net rather than on portable supports.

6. Adoption of standard languages oriented to the logic structure of the document.

7. Institution of a distributed digital legal deposit for documents distributed on the net.

The extension and strengthening of document distribution on the net will be one of the main means of guaranteeing the transmission to future generations of at least a part of the present and future digital network. However, one could object that it is risky to become too dependent on something so hazardous and fragile as telematic networks. This is certainly true, but is it not likewise true for other types of networks that we cannot help using, such as electric and telephonic networks?

Notes

[1] <ridi@aib.it> coordinator AIB-WEB <http://www.aib.it>. Personal homepage <http://www.burioni.it/forum/ridi>

[2] Adaptation from "Il retaggio multimediale fra hardware, software e politiche culturali", in: *L'automazione delle biblioteche nel Veneto: l'irruzione della multimedialità*, atti del nono Seminario Angela Vinay, 5 Dicembre 1997, ed. by C. Rabitti, Fondazione scientifica Querini Stampalia, Venezia, 1999: 121-124, or <http://www.aib.it/aib/sezioni/veneto/ridi.htm>. English translation by Chris Whitehead.

[3] Here I will exclusively deal with the theme of the preservation of electronic documents, independently from the fact that they may have been created directly in a digital environment or as a result of the acquisition of paper originals. For an overview of the theme of digitization as a form of paper document preservation, see Shoaf 1996: 223-239.

[4] On the distinction between "document" and "relic" ("cimelio") in the library see Serrai 1980: 151-154 ("the difference between the document and the relic is that the latter is no longer sought or consulted for the symbols it contains, but for the material and formal characteristics of the package which acts as a support to the linguistic symbols"), where, on pages 83-84, the distinction between "literary unit" (the work), "bibliographical unit" (the edition) and the single document (the exemplar) is made.

[5] It goes without saying that the vision of a modern typographic impression producing absolutely identical exemplars is, however pragmatically accepted, a *fictio*.

⁶ See Ridi 1998: 12-19.

⁷ See Gregory & Morelli (eds.) 1994 (in particular the essays by D. Schüller, L. Duranti, Ch.H. Dollar, H. Zemanek & P. Ridolfi); Rothenberg 1995: 16-21; Blasi 1997.

⁸ "The concept of conservation cannot signify other than the acceptance and maintenance of that which is held to be important and useful, in that we ourselves are part of a certain civilisation; without the ingenuous presumption of having our Pantheons contain the whole picture of the present civilisation for the use of future generations. [...] No civilisation is a faithful interpreter of itself in the creation of future projections; no civilisation can turn itself into a museum. But above all such 'self musealisation' cannot be effected by way of the accumulation and depositing of all that is produced, printed, said, represented, in order to avoid the future from being possessed of a partial image of this epoch." Serrai 1980.: 29-30.
"In every literary society what has been written or all received written material is never entirely conserved. Above all, those societies which use writing extensively and produce large masses of testimonials provide for the destruction of a large part of the same. This occurred in The Roman world at the apogee of its process of literacy, between the first and second centuries AD.; it occurred in modern Europe; it occurs today." (Petrucci 1993: 147-152).
"Inevitably, every generation chooses – more or less consciously – among the infinite quantities of information it manipulates that subset worthy of being transmitted to subsequent generations. It is in the interest – and it is the duty – of all, that such an operation is executed with politically democratic and technically reliable criteria. The task of librarians is to assist in organising and rendering available quantities of information in a complete and efficient way, so that the choice is not distorted by the scarce visibility of certain data or by the over-exhibition of others; but it is utopian to think that Internet today or any other technology tomorrow can exempt librarians and citizens from such ineluctable tasks." Ridi 1996: 203-204.

⁹ In itself a file is not a document. It is only the *description* of a document, which becomes real only when interpreted by the program which produced it. Without this program (or a software equivalent) the document remains prisoner of its own encoding. Rothenberg 1995: 18. The italics are Rothenberg's.

¹⁰ Rothenberg 1995: 19.

¹¹ Even the hypothesis of translating the informative content into progressively current standards encounters great obstacles in the incommensurateness between language and software. See Rothenberg 1995: 19.

¹² "A function which can perhaps be undertaken in the best way by the library in a new acceptation of the concept of *philology*. Even those of us who have witnessed first the appearance and then the explosion of the desk-computer in our work and research organisation, may not to be able to read electronically what we wrote only a few years ago with what now are obsolete machines and programs. Why not imagine that library technology may also turn into *computer archaeology*, that is, a means of documenting the survival of single exemplars of machines and programs able to read electronic supports printed or produced through technologies which have since become obsolete?" See Innocenti 1997: 55-71 (68). (The italics are mine).

[13] A particular concept of "*philology*", that is of the care of the integrity of a text, to which the library is structurally deputised, in that its task is to conserve the testimonials of that text". (See Innocenti 1997: 59. The italics are mine).

[14] Relief, in my opinion partial and non-resolving, could come from the use of "the so-called emulator programs which allow pieces of software written for one machine to run on another (for example a computer of the past)" (Blasi *ib*).

[15] For a rapid overview of the principal formats available for the realisation of digital libraries see Metitieri & Ridi 1998: 172-178.

[16] Even the blind can read it, thanks to audio interfaces which interpret the logic structure of the document. "Fortunately, Hypertext Markup Language (HTML) – the encoding system used to prepare a text for the World Wide Web – was designed to capture the structure of documents. If it were used as originally intended, the same electronic source could be rendered in fine detail on a printer, at lower resolution on a screen, in spoken language for functionally blind users, and in myriad other ways to suit individual preferences. Unfortunately, HTML is steadily evolving under commercial pressure to make it possible to design purely visual Web pages that cannot be used at all, unless one can see the color graphics and rapidly download large images. This current rush to design Web pages that can be properly viewed only with the most popular programs and standard displays, and that lack important structural information, risks undermining the usefulness of the documents archived on the Internet." (Raman 1997/3: 41-73), or <http://www.sciam.com/0397issue/0397raman.html>).

[17] See Kahle 1997, <http://www.sciam.com/0397issue/0397kahle.html>.

[18] UBC and UAP are core programmes of IFLA (International Federation of Library Associations). See <http://ifla.inist.fr/VI/index.htm>.

[19] "For the moment no convincing solutions for the long-term archiving of digital format documents have been advanced. Legal deposits for this type of documents are being discussed in many countries, but we are still far from a convincing and economic solution." (Pettinati 1997: 72-85) (75).

[20] See Ridi 1996: 63-65.

[21] See Neavill & Sheble 1995: 13-21; Barnes 1997: 404-415.

[22] See Haynes & Streatfield: 1998, <http://www.ariadne.ac.uk/issue15/digital>.

[23] The acronym PURL stands for a Persistent URL, that is, an Internet address which remains unchanged even when the associated document shifts into cyberspace, thanks to the "triangulation" guaranteed by one or more agencies that control the migrations of a given set of documents, thus saving the users tiring treasure hunts. In the same institutional entity, the marriage of the digital legal deposit with the management of the relative PURLs could lead to the creation of a modality of "publication" on the net capable of convincing of its stability even the "legislator" who is the most skeptical about technological innovations. See *PURL frequently asked questions*, <http://purl.oclc.org/OCLC/PURL/FAQ>.

References

BARNES, J.H.
1997 "One giant leap, one small step: Continuing the migration to electronic journals", *Library trends*, XLV, 3.

BLASI, G.
1997 "E' possibile una biblioteca multimediale?", *Golem*, 11/12/14.
<http://www.enel.it/it/enel/magazine/golem/ArchivioGolem/Golem11/links.htm>
<http://www.enel.it/it/enel/magazine/golem/ArchivioGolem/Golem12/links.htm>
<http://www.enel.it/it/enel/magazine/golem/ArchivioGolem/Golem14/links.htm>

COCHETTI, M. (ED.)
1993 *Mercurius in trivio. Studi di bibliografia e di biblioteconomia per Alfredo Serrai nel Sessantesimo compleanno (20 novembre 1992)*, Roma: Bulzoni.

GALLUZZI, P. & P.A. VALENTINO (EDS.)
1997 *I formati della memoria. Beni culturali e nuove tecnologie alle soglie del terzo millennio*, Firenze: Giunti.

GREGORY, T. & M. MORELLI
1994 *L'eclisse delle memorie*, preface by G. Salvini, Roma-Bari: Laterza.

HAYNES, D. & D. STREATFIELD
1998 "A national co-ordinating body for digital archiving?", *Ariadne*, 15.
<http://www.ariadne.ac.uk/issue15/digital/>.

INNOCENTI, P.
1997 "Tecnologie informatiche e struttura tradizionale della biblioteca", in Galluzzi & Valentino 1997: 55-71 (68).

KAHLE, B.
1997 "Preserving the Internet", in *The Internet: Fulfilling the Promise*, special report, "Scientific American", CCLXXVI, 3.
<http://www.sciam.com/0397issue/0397kahle.html>.

METITIERI, F. & R. RIDI
1998 Ricerche *bibliografiche in Internet. Strumenti e strategie di ricerca, OPAC e biblioteche virtuali*, Milano: Apogeo.

NEAVILL, B. & M.A., SHEBLE
1995 "Archiving electronic journals", *Serials review*, XII, 4.

PETRUCCI, A.
1993 "Logiche della conservazione e pratiche conoscitive", in Cochetti 1993: 147-152 (147).

PETTINATI, C.
1997 "La biblioteca virtuale: problemi e opportunità", in Galluzzi &. Valentino 1997: 72-85 (75).

RAMAN, T.V.
1997 "Netsurfing without a monitor", in *The Internet: Fulfilling the Promise*, special report, "Scientific American", CCLXXVI, 3.
<http://www.sciam.com/0397issue/0397raman.html>).

RIDI, R.
1996 *Internet in biblioteca*, Milano: Editrice Bibliografica.
1998 "Dal canone alla rete: il ruolo del bibliotecario nell'organizzazione del sapere digitale", *Biblioteche oggi*, XVI/5.

ROTHENBERG, J.
1995 "La conservazione dei documenti digitali", *Le scienze*, LIV, 319.

SERRAI, A.
1980 *Sistemi bibliotecari e meccanismi catalografici*, Roma: Bulzoni.

SHOAF, E.C.
1996 "Preservation and digitization: trends and implications", *Advances in librarianship*, XX.

Michele Santoro[1]

LIBRARIES: OUR FUTURE PRESERVED

> *If history is any guide, the future will be populated with a more varied and complicated collection of forms and institutions than the present, and we are likely to find it no less uncanny for what it preserves than for what it alters.*
> Geoffrey Nunberg

1. Preservation and libraries today

What is a library? Everybody knows, of course, what a library is, but when the question is asked, the first idea that comes to our minds is a place where books are collected and preserved. This is a first definition of library. However, this definition is brief and superficial: it's not adequate to represent either the technical peculiarities or the specific aims of a library. Therefore, it is necessary to introduce a detailed definition of "library", assuming that it is "an organized collection of books and other materials (manuscripts, printed, audio-visuals, electronics) available for reading, reference and loan" (See Serrai 1983)

Of course, if we compare the first definition to the second, there are remarkable differences. On the one hand, the second definition increases the range of documentation preserved in a library. On the other, it realizes a "dynamic" vision, where users' requests are completely satisfied by several services that overcome the "static" frame whereby a library is intended as a simple storage overflowing with books.

Therefore, the latter is a much more satisfying definition. It refers to some crucial aspects of the library activity as well as to the conceptual assumptions that are at the basis of librarianship. This discipline concerns the knowledge and the techniques necessary to establish, order and manage a documentary collection. However, even adopting the second definition, something is lost, that is, the idea of preservation, or the ability, related to any documentary collection, to be preserved unchanged.

We are facing a crucial point regarding not only the everyday life of libraries, but their millenary history, too, the long path from the first collections of clay tablets to the actual multimedia dimensions. "A book is only a book", said an expert on Medieval libraries, "but two books are the beginning of a library": every time a library or a collection is formed, it goes on automatically and is constitutionally voted to be passed on to future generations.

Therefore, preservation is something more than a technical feature, or an aspect that defines a library better: it is a basic element, genetically bound to libraries. Nevertheless, it seems that today this element, this "hard point" of a library image, is confined to a minor role. According to many librarians, the field of preservation is like the selected world of a limited circle of scholars who, in their closed rooms, celebrate a kind of ritual for the perpetuation of a secluded and formal type of knowledge. As a result, our old libraries, rich of memories of the past, are considered with a conceited and annoying air. Such considerations come from those embracing the most fashionable ideas in the library world; for example, those who use expressions such as library without walls, global library, logic library, or even meta-library to describe the new informational frontiers; or those who often exalt the idea of an easy access to information by using documents available on the web, against the idea of owning, acquiring and preserving bibliographic materials in libraries.

On the contrary, "ownership", which means systematic management of documentation,[2] symbolizes the essence of preservation, the constituent root of each documentary set. Probably, the enthusiasm toward the innovative frontiers of the virtual library, or the fascination for dazzling information technology tools[3] might have driven us to neglect the real nature of preservation. But today even the most enthusiastic supporters of these views are facing a new and dramatic event: the possibility, not at all remote, that electronic documents – either produced in digital format or converted from a printed one – might be lost.

Many specialists have pointed out not only the weakness and volatility of digital data, but also the fast obsolescence of computer systems. In different countries, many task forces are working to find solutions to this problem.[4] In this context, it would be very difficult to deal with technical aspects or to consider different hypotheses in detail. So, we would like to make just some remarks "from a library point of view", in a period in which libraries are facing crucial challenges for both their image and their activities.[5]

2. Production, preservation and circulation in library history

The library, as Alfredo Serrai wrote, was born when objects – like the physical media to record symbols that replaced oral communication – were collected. These objects are the documents, from clay tablets to digital resources. The library is a storage of symbols. Together with the biological memory of the species and with the cerebral memory of the individual, the library should be thought as a collective memory of everyday experience, as well as of the scientific and cultural life of both individuals and societies (Serrai 1980: 39-40).

Therefore, if the library represents a deeper collective memory, it can carry out its own task through the interconnected functions of *production*, *preservation* and *circulation* of knowledge. In particular, as Pietro Rossi pointed out , preservation implies the two other functions, since it takes its assumption from the production and, at the same time, is essential to the circulation of knowledge (Rossi 1990: V). It is needless to say that the strong interconnection between these functions is the basis for all cultural events occurring in society. However, it is interesting to note that these functions have a practical application in such specific places as museums, archives and, in particular, libraries, which are institutionally devoted to realize them in order to turn a conceptual hypothesis into a technical role.

The difference is clear: when we no longer speak of production, preservation and circulation of *knowledge* but of *documents*, we shift to a more operative and technical dimension, that is, oneconcerning the domain of librarianship. Nevertheless, studying in depth the concept of preservation from a library point of view, doesn't mean excluding the cultural aspects related to it: in other words, all those events – over the centuries, inside and outside libraries – which helped to preserve knowledge for future generations. This view has always acknowledged the importance of preserving all produced documents as much as possible. Therefore, on the one hand, the history of preservation is strongly related to the "history of knowledge"; on the other hand, this history is connected with the different media used to spread and preserve knowledge. In this respect, the history of books and libraries is related to the world "of ancient philosophical schools, of medieval *studia*, of 17th and 18th century academies and scientific societies, of 19th century universities, and of laboratories and research centers inside or outside modern universities" (*Ib*.: VII). Likewise, a study on new electronic formats and their preservation should include an analysis of the technological, cultural and social context in which those formats have been produced, as well as inquiries into the digital world in which we live.

In this context, the term "preservation" should be carefully considered. In fact, as a recent report explains, "preservation includes conservation", that is, "the reactive and proactive treatment of library material to strengthen them physically or stabilize chemically, thus sustaining their survival as long as they are needed in the original form".[6] In other words, conservation is used with a more technical connotation; it deals with the problems related to the restoration of damaged documents.[7] On the contrary, preservation has a more general meaning; it indicates the typical role of libraries of the safeguard of documents to be handed down to posterity.

If we adopt this meaning, we can look at the whole history of libraries not only as a simple development of library collections, but also as a diachronic evolution of methods for organizing documents. This is an important distinction, which makes it possible to shift from a traditional "history of libraries" – or a simple description of outward aspects or events – to a real "history of librarianship", which underlines the methods and the techniques used during the ages to make a better use of documents.[8] A search on preservation would allow one to overcome the limits of a narrower vision of restoration and care; on the other hand, it might be integrated in a larger context where the specific issues of librarianship meet the cultural aspects related to the preservation of knowledge. Such a search can give us an accurate view of our documentary history, which, at the same time, is our cultural and intellectual history.[9]

3. A brief history of library preservation

If we want to go back to the origins of libraries, according to tradition flourished in Mesopotamia from the third millennium B.C.,[10] we can notice that "the dawn of civilization" produced several libraries devoted to the preservation of knowledge. It is interesting to point out that these libraries used accurate and surprisingly modern criteria of preservation and organization. For example, in the Assurbanipal collection – the most famous because it was recovered almost integral – the tablets were preserved inside clay vases orderly aligned on the base of a definite and systematic division. As a matter of fact, the tablets were arranged in the different rooms according to their contents;[11] a label on the tablets identified the vases, the shelf and the room where they were arranged. A sort of topographical catalogue listed the content of each room.

This clearly shows a first way of understanding the link between preservation and use: on the one hand, suitable rules for preservation were used; on the other, an effective system for organizing and retrieving documents was discovered.

This system – as far as we know – didn't change when a new documentary medium appeared: the papyrus roll. On the contrary, it developed in ancient times with similar features. In Egyptian libraries the rolls were preserved inside vases placed in niches or on shelves, according to a suitable order (Sperry 1957: 145-155). We are also aware that such preservation criteria were used in Micene and Pilo's palaces (Harris 1984: 33). Finally, we know that the great Alexandrian library was based on a similar model, keeping together an adequate preservation and an effective saving system of a great number of scrolls.[12] O'Donnell (1998: 33), among others, underlines the importance of "the pigeonholes into which the papyrus scrolls at Alexandria were to fit [...]: this economical and easily managed form of packaging would speed the access readers wanted".

However, this preservation system was strictly linked with the cultural, social and symbolic functions of the greatest library in ancient times. On the one hand, the Alexandrian library met the requirements of Hellenistic sovereigns of "owning, *hic et nunc*, the knowledge of all ages and of the whole *oikouméne*" (Cavallo 1990: 34); it is, indeed, organized in "storage-rooms" that guarantee the best preservation of the acquired volumes. On the other hand, it became a place of production and revision of knowledge on the part of the *élite* of scholars, philologists and poets who used it. As a result, tools and techniques for a better preservation and use of the documents were introduced: as Hans Wellisch wrote, "it forged for the first time the bibliographic tools that are still used today to create order out of the chaos of a large and growing collection of books – alphabetical arrangement of authors' names, accompanied by the titles of their works; systematic subject catalogs, subdivided by authors' names and titles; and meticulous and physical descriptions of books and other items" (Wellisch 1999: 21).

The Roman world gave libraries a stronger "public" position , by opening them to all "learned" citizens, to everybody who was able to use them for both study and pleasure.[13] The ability of preservation and document retrieval was improved by shelving the books "on elevated bookcases arranged inside niches": "a method of preservation", wrote Guglielmo Cavallo, "inspired to precise rules on the distribution of knowledge, on economy and functionality" (Cavallo 1990: 41).

The shift from ancient times to the Middle ages was a crucial event in the history of the preservation of knowledge. In fact, a huge quantity of knowledge had already been lost at that time;[14] and it was only in the late ancient world that mechanisms for preservation were figured out and developed.[15]

Gradually, monasteries, cathedrals and courts gave rise to that core of books which would secure the preservation and the transmission of knowledge.[16] However, this happened also thanks to the discovery of a new important writing material: the parchment. Its presence meant the definitive shift from roll to codex. Thanks to its strength, its easy handling, and its non-linear way of reading,[17] the parchment codex became the key medium onto which knowledge was transferred.

The function of production was strongly exalted because the convent communities – on the basis of the Benedictine rule – were moved to copy the codices they owned. Nevertheless, in that period the link between preservation and use that was typical of ancient libraries was broken. The collections were restricted to an internal use, that is, to the practical and spiritual needs of the religious communities; thus, the arrangement of books in the "armaria" placed in the chorus, in the refectory, in the sacristy or in the cells testify to a form of care strictly linked to the different stages of the monks' daily life.

In the following centuries, starting from the "renaissance of the 12th century", the previous model of preservation, oriented to the care of books rather than their use, came to a crisis. In this period, the greater number of available volumes enabled a wider circulation of knowledge and a larger use of libraries. This produced a radical change in the methods of shelving, putting the most requested books in chain on the pews. At this time, the purpose of the collections was reference- rather than preservation-oriented.

The next step is related to the discovery of printing, and to the extraordinary transformations it brought about in every social and cultural field.[18] Starting from the second half of the 15th century, the increase of books produced big changes in the life of libraries.[19] "The library", in other words, "became a dynamic rather than a static institution, a place not so much of revealed truth as of growth, change, and variety" (S.O. Thompson 1999: 509).

The problem of increasing number of books flowing into libraries was faced by introducing great architectural changes: the library was provided with a big room-storage; and the books were arranged on large shelves that covered the whole wall. In this way, books became not only objects to preserve but also objects to show, a real patrimony available for the users (Boriani 1984: 8-22; Solitine 1998: 41-91).

Starting with Gutenberg, the idea of preservation was of course linked to that of serial production, which was able to save knowledge thanks to a large number of available copies. This "documentary overload" forced the adoption of strict rules concerning physical and conceptual organization: on the one hand, more functional models of location were introduced; on the other hand, the library catalogues – alphabetic or systematic – were improved (Rouse & Rouse 1979: 24-26; Carpenter 1999: 108). Another crucial event was the birth of great bibliographies, among which the Conrad Gesner's *Bibliotheca universalis* is worth remembering: it listed and described all the publications available at his time.[20]

Therefore, in that period the idea of a universal bibliographic control took shape: that is, the need "to make universally available […] the bibliographic records of the publication produced in every country".[21] This is a key aspect, not only for the history of bibliography, but also for library preservation. In fact, a wide recording of publications makes knowledge available, and, consequently, more easily preserved.

Between the 18th and 19th century, in the different European countries, the legal deposit became a fundamental rule; it forced all printers or publishers to give one copy of every book they produced to the most important library in the nation.

This increased the collections stored in libraries, which had already been enriched by the books received from the dissolution of religious orders. It was in this period that National libraries appeared. In a short time, they assumed important functions: on the one hand, they became responsible for the acquisition and preservation of all documents published in their countries; on the other, they had the task to make up national bibliographies.

Recent history is characterised by the enormous increase in information available not only on paper but also on digital formats. Preservation criteria have changed, since digital documents undergo the highest levels of deterioration and obsolescence.

4. Library preservation in the digital world

In the last ten years, the shift from paper to electronic texts produced a large amount of resources available in digital format, either on physical media (floppy disk, CD-ROM, DVD), or in a non-material form (online data-banks, Internet resources). The "media revolution" is producing effects never achieved in the past. This revolution has not only increased the possibility of accessing and using the information, but it has also modified our approach to reality, producing transformations both in the social and in the psychological field.[22]

Therefore, this revolution seems to be crucial in our world. In particular libraries are deeply involved in these changes.[23] They are facing new kinds of information,[24] linked no more to physical media, but freely available on telematic networks: this information must now be selected, organised and preserved for the users.

So, libraries have to handle new functions. Firstly, the *choice* of a useful range of information among that available on the Internet. Secondly, the *validation* of such information, that is, its scholarly reliability. Thirdly, the *organisation* of this information according to suitable cataloguing criteria. Last but not least, libraries have to face adequate procedures of *preservation*, because "without preservation, access become impossible, and collections decay and disintegrate" (Rothenberg 1998).

The shift of a large number of documents from paper to digital format is one of the basic purposes of digital libraries. Among the advantages of digitisation many people include preservation; in fact, they think that the translation into digital format could lead to an indefinite and total preservation of documents.[25]

This is not necessarily true. As Abby Smith writes, "digitisation is not preservation – at least not yet [...]. Digital resources are at their best when facilitating access to information, and weakest when assigned the traditional library responsibility of preservation" (Smith 1999).

As a matter of fact, the life span of electronic media is very short compared to paper. A research conducted by the National Media Lab has shown that magnetic tapes, disks and CD-ROMs have relatively short lives; a VHS tape becomes unreliable after ten years, and average-quality CD-ROMs are unreliable after only five years; hardware, software, and operating systems become obsolete in few years;[26] in the end, the Internet documents have the shortest lifetime: according to

Brewster Kahle (1998: 39), the average life expectancy of a web page is roughly 70 days.

Due to this issue, in the last ten years there have been several research projects on strategies of preservation of digital documents. These strategies consist in the production of "hard copies", in other words in printing the digital materials; in preserving – as in a museum – obsolete hardware and software; in *refreshing*, that is, transferring documents from old onto new media; in the *reliance on standards*, that is, the shift to new software sharing the same paradigms as the old one; in the *migration*, that is, the systematic shift of documents onto new hardware and software before the old ones become obsolete; and, eventually, in the *emulation,* which, as Jeff Rothenberg wrote, is "an approach to enable the emulation of obsolete systems on future, unknown systems, so that a digital document's original software can be run in the future despite being obsolete" (Rothenberg 1998).

There have been many discussions on the validity of such strategies (Bearman 1999). However, at least the last two strategies are clearly a right method for digital preservation; particularly if, together with them, we could use the metadata.

The library community is beginning to see the usefulness of metadata, not just for resource discovery, but as a help to the ongoing management of digital – specifically networked – resources, including preservation (Day 1997). For example, it is important to identify what metadata would be needed to enable the emulation of digital information created on obsolete hardware and software platforms; collecting metadata would be also an important part of migration strategies (Day & Beagrie 1998).

The topic of metadata leads us to one of the crucial points that libraries are facing today: on the one hand, the large number of useful information available on the web; on the other, their volatility, since it is easy to lose them just after few weeks. Provided that the net is an important source for information retrieval, the subject of the preservation of Internet resources becomes fundamental for librarians, and it has to be seriously faced.

In this context, there are well-known projects like that by Brewster Kahle that aim at archiving all the information present on the web (Kahle 1997). We don't want to speak about the evident utopian and superficial aspects of the project. Nevertheless, it is worth underlining that this project is hardly plausible. In fact these archives, if devoted to a documentary goal, cannot receive every kind of information available on the web indiscriminately; a selection among more than a million of resources is necessary in order to separate the useful and the convenient information from the vain, useless, or even harmful ones.[27]

This and other similar projects are not suitable for the preservation of the Internet documents. Who can assume this task, which seems so onerous not only in financial terms, but also because it would mean observing all the issues underlined before (right location of the sources, validation of the acquired documents, their organisation and preservation)? Probably, National libraries are the only institutions able to play such a demanding task.

For example, the Pandora Project of the National Library of Australia set out on this path.[28] After the creation of a small "proof of concept" archive, and of the development of a "national model", the Library has worked out a number of strategies to archive network documents. They include all the functions mentioned above: the *identification* of items to be archived in time before they disappear; their *selection*, to avoid the management of documents with a low research value; the accurate *search* of these items through the different tools available, especially the metadata; the *validation*, that is, the warrant that the record stored is accurate and that it will keep true to the original. In the end, the certainty that the document could be exactly located; particularly through the attribution of a PURL (*Permanent URL, Uniform Resource Locator*), but also on the basis of other possibilities, for example DOI (*Digital Object Identifier*) or URN (*Uniform Resource Name*).

Such a matter fits in the historical path of libraries devoted to the preservation and use of knowledge. The involvement of National libraries could meet the requisites of accuracy and bibliographic reliability that are essential to a right preservation of documents. Therefore, the need to make choices in the big Internet store means the end of the idea of a universal bibliographic control – the total recording of all publications, both printed and digital, available in the world. This idea, as Mauro Guerrini suggests, could be replaced by that of a "national bibliographic control" (Guerrini 1999: 62). In fact, National libraries will be increasingly assigned preservation tasks, including the new tasks of individuation, selection and description of digital documents.

So, we would like to end this paper with Abby Smith's words:

> The challenge of the future tense for preservation professionals is to continue to look beyond the object to the medium, and beyond the medium to the creator and the user, and embrace responsibility for long-term custody of all forms of recorded information to ensure continued access to them. (Smith 1998)

Notes

[1] Department of Economics' Library, University of Bologna, e-mail: santoro@spbo.unibo.it. In this paper all the translations from Italian texts are ours.

[2] See Crasta 1991: 43-78; Geretto 1991: 79-119; Carotti 1997; Solimine 1999.

[3] On this topic see Santoro 1999: 85-95.

[4] See, among others, *Preserving digital information. Report of the Task Force on Archiving of Digital Information*, commissioned by The Commission of Preservation and Access and The Research Library Group, <http://www.rlg.org/ArchTF/tfadi.index.htm>; Beagrie & Greenstein 1998. A good collection of resources on this topic has been prepared by De Robbio (1998).

[5] See Smith 1998.

[6] *What is preservation?* in *Preserving library materials*, UCDS Library Preservation Department, <http://orpheus.ucsd.edu/preservation/whatspre.html>. In this report, a general definition of the term is provided: "Preservation, by definition, is activities associated with maintaining library and archival materials for use either in their original physical form or in some other usable way". See also Smith 1998.

[7] See, among others, Revelli 1996.

[8] On the topic see Danesi 1985: 153-160; Serrai 1989: 187-189; Serrai. 1992: 217-224 (both collected in Serrai 1994: 93-97); Schneiders & Richards 1977.

[9] For this perspective, see Cloonan 1993: 594-605.

[10] Milkau & Leyh (ed.) 1940; Thompson 1940; Hessel 1955; Thompson 1977; Harris 1984.

[11] Samurin 1964-1967; Weitemeyer 1956: 227; Liverani: 499-513.

[12] Pasquali 1930: 942-969; Canfora: 1988: 7.; Canfora 1990; Cavallo 1990a: VIII; Cavallo 1990a: 29-67; Jacob 1996: 57-83.

[13] About Roman libraries see Pasquali 1930: 944 sg.; Cavallo 1990a: 38-45; Fedeli 1988: 31-64.

[14] See Canfora 1974.

[15] Cavallo (1990a: 45) points out that it would be a big mistake to believe that "all the heritage of the works from ancient times have been handed down almost integral-

ly throughout the second century after Christ and that, starting from that age, those works have been overturned by the general crisis of the ancient world [...]. Instead, the heritage of knowledge, that the late ancient times were facing, was already thinned, or simply forgotten or lost during the last century; rather, it was just the late ancient world who understood the crisis and developed mechanisms for the preservation of the works still available". On this topic, see also Petrucci 1993: 147.

[16] See particularly Christ 1940: 234-498; Thompson 1957; Petrucci 1983: 527-554; Cavallo (ed.) 1989.

[17] O'Donnell (1998: 54) summarizes the capabilities of codex in the following way: "First, since its size was limited only by the strength of the user (or the user's furniture), much more material could be contained in a single unit. Second, the codex could be taken apart, put together, and rearranged at will. This meant that several different authors and titles could be combined and recombined with minimal difficulty. Third, and of greatest importance, nonlinear access to the material in the volume was possible. By this I mean simply that readers did not need to shuffle through every page from beginning to end to find quickly what they sought. With appropriate indexing or dumb luck they could pop the book open in the middle and quickly find what they were looking for".

[18] See particularly Febvre & Martin 1958; McLuhan 1964; Eisenstein 1979.

[19] See Petrucci (ed.) 1977; Petrucci (ed.) 1979.

[20] Balsamo 1984 (particularly p. 28 and p. 38); Serrai 1990.

[21] Solitine 1995: 5; see also Davinson 1975.

[22] See, among others, Bolter 1986; Turkle 1984; *Id.* 1996; De Kerckhove 1995.

[23] On this subject see Santoro 1998: 303-322.

[24] *What is information? A discussion from the Cristal-Ed listserv*, November 1997, <http://lrs.stcloudstate.edu/cim/courses/im577/infodef.html>.

[25] "Digitization may come to be regarded as a *panacea* for all of the real and imagined problems libraries now face in connection with the preservation of physical collections: the growing need for storage space, the deterioration of books due to acid paper, and the rising cost of library operation" (Lehmann 1996: 309).

[26] See Marcum 1998.

[27] "Like Shakespeare's Cleopatra, the World Wide Web is 'infinite in variety'. Anyone who has spent more than a modicum of time surfing the Web has encountered the good, the bad, and the ugly among is offering" (Rettig 1996).

[28] The project is available at the URL <http://pandora.nla.gov.au/index.html>.

References

AA.VV.
1997 *What is Information? A Discussion from the Cristal-Ed listserv*, November 1997, <http://lrs.stcloudstate.edu/cim/courses/im577/infodef.html>.

AA.VV.
"What is preservation?", in *Preserving Library Materials*, UCDS Library Preservation Department.

AA.V.V.
1996 *Le pouvoir des bibliothèques. La mémoire des livres en Occident*, sous la direction de M. Baratin et Ch. Jacob, Paris: Albin Michel.

ACCARISI, M. & M. BELOTTI
1984 *Abitare le biblioteche. Arredo e organizzazione degli spazi nella biblioteca pubblica*, Roma: Oberon.

BALSAMO, L.
1984 *La bibliografia. Storia di una tradizione*, Firenze: Sansoni.

BEAGRIE, N. & D. GREENSTEIN
1998 *A Strategic Policy Framework for Creating and Preserving Digital Collections, Arts and Humanities Data Service*, London: King's College.

BEARMAN, D.
1999 "Reality and chimeras in the preservation of electronic records", *D-Lib Magazine*, 5, 5, <http://www.dlib.org/dlib/april99/bearman/04bearman.html>.

BOLTER, J.D.
1986 *Turing's man*, Harmondsworth: Penguin Books.

BORIANI, M.
1984 "Conservazione e accesso al patrimonio librario nella storia dello spazio delle biblioteche", in Accarisi & Belotti 1984: 8-22.

CANFORA, L.
1974 *Conservazione e perdita dei classici*, Padova: Antenore.
1988 "Le biblioteche ellenistiche", in Cavallo (ed.) 1988.

CAROTTI, C.
1997 *Costruzione e sviluppo delle raccolte*, Roma: Associazione Italiana Biblioteche.

CARPENTER, M.
1999 "Catalogs and cataloging", in Wiegand &. Davis (eds.) 1999.

CAVALLO, G.
1988 "Introduzione" in Cavallo (ed.) 1988: VIII
1990a "Cultura scritta e conservazione del sapere: dalla Grecia antica all'Occidente medievale", in Rossi (ed.) 1990: 29-67.
1990b *La biblioteca scomparsa*, Palermo: Sellerio.

CAVALLO G. (ED.)
1988 *Le biblioteche nel mondo antico e medievale*, Roma-Bari: Laterza.
1989 *Libri e lettori nel Medioevo. Guida storica e critica*, Roma-Bari: Laterza.

CHRIST, K.
1940 "Das Mittelalter", in *Handbuch der Bibliothekswissenschaft*, founded by F. Milkau e G. Leyh, Leipzig: Harrasowitz.

CLOONAN, M.V.
1993 "The preservation of knowledge", in *Library Trends*, 41, 4: 594-605.

COCHETTI M.
1993 *Mercurius in trivio. Studi di bibliografia e biblioteconomia in onore di Alfredo Serrai nel 60° compleanno*, Roma: Bulzoni.

CRASTA, M.
1991 "La formazione delle raccolte", in Geretto (ed.) 1991: 43-78

DANESI, D.
1985 "Dalla storia delle biblioteche alla storia della biblioteconomia", *Bollettino d'Informazioni AIB*, 25, 2: 153-160.

DAVINSON, D.E.
1975 *Bibliographic Control*, London: Bingley.

DAY, M.
1997 "Extending metadata for digital preservation", *Ariadne*, 9, May. <http://www.ariadne.ac.uk/issue9/metadata>.

DAY, M. & N. BEAGRIE
1998 "Sixth DELOS Workshop - Preservation of digital information, June 17-19, 1998, Tomar, Portugal", *D-Lib Magazine*, July/August 1998, <http://www.dlib.org/dlib/july98/07clips.html#DELOS>.

DE KERCKHOVE, D.
1995 *The Skin of Culture*, Toronto: Somerville House.

DE ROBBIO, A.
1998 *Conservazione di documenti elettronici*, <http://www.math.unipd.it/~derobbio/preserv.htm>

EISENSTEIN, E.L.
1979 *The Printing Press as an Agent of Change. Communication and Cultural Transformation in Early Modern Europe*, Cambridge: Cambridge University Press.

FEBVRE, L. & H.-J. MARTIN
1958 *L'apparition du livre*, Paris: Albin Michel.

FEDELI, P.
1988 "Biblioteche private e pubbliche a Roma e nel mondo romano", in Cavallo 1988: 31-64.

FOGLIENI, O.
1999 *Bibliotecario nel 2000. Come cambia la professione nell'era digitale*, Milano: Editrice Bibliografica.

GERETTO, P.
1991 "La gestione delle raccolte", in Geretto (ed.) 1991: 79-119.

GERETTO, P. (ED.)
1991 *Lineamenti di bibliotecononomia,* Firenze: La Nuova Italia Scientifica.

GUERRINI, M.
1999 "Catalogare le risorse elettroniche. Lo standard ISBD (ER)", *Biblioteche oggi*, 17, 1, <http://www.burioni.it/forum/isbder.htm>.

HARRIS, M.H.
1984 *History of Libraries in the Western World*, Metuchen-London: The Scarecrow Press. Revised edition of E.D. Johnson, *History of libraries in the western world*, 3rd ed. 1976.

HESSEL, A.
1995 *A History of Library*, New Brunswick: The Scarecrow Press.

JACOB, CH.
1996 "Navigations Alexandrines", in AA.VV. 1996.

KAHLE, B.
1997 "Archiving the Internet", *Scientific American*, March, <http://www.archive.org/sciam_article.html>.
1998 "Setting the stage: summary of the initial discussion", in McLean & Davis 1998.

LEHMANN, K.-D.
1996 "Making the transitory permanent: the intellectual heritage in a digitized world of knowledge", in *Books, Bricks and Bytes*: issued as a volume 125, number 4 of the Proceedings of the American Academy of Arts and Sciences, Cambridge (MA): Daedalus.

LIVERANI, M.
1976 *L'alba della civiltà*, v. 3: *Il pensiero*, Torino: UTET: 499-513.

MARCUM, D.
1998 *The Great Digital Crisis. Letter to the Washington Post*, Wednesday, January 21.

MCLEAN, M. & B.H DAVIS (EDS.)
1998 *Time & Bits: Managing Digital Continuity*, Santa Monica: The Paul Getty Trust.

MCLUHAN, M.
1964 *The Gutenberg Galaxy. The Making of Typographic Man*, New York: A Signet Book.

MILKAU, F. & G. LEYH (ED.)
1940 *Geschichte der Bibliotheken*, 3rd volume, *Handbuch der Bibliothekswissenschaft*, Leipzig: Harrasowitz.

O'Donnell, J.
1998 *Avatars of the Words. From Papyrus to Cyberspace*, Cambridge (MA): Harvard University Press.

Pasquali, G.
1930 "Biblioteca", *in Enciclopedia Italiana*, vol. VI, Roma: Istituto dell'Enciclopedia Italiana: 942-969.

Petrucci, A. (ed.)
1977 *Libri, editori e pubblico nell'Europa moderna*, Roma-Bari: Laterza.
1979 *Libri, scrittura e pubblico nel Rinascimento*, Roma-Bari: Laterza.
1983 "Le biblioteche antiche", in *Letteratura italiana*, II, *Produzione e consumo*, Torino: Einaudi: 527-554
1993 "Logiche della conservazione e pratiche conoscitive", in Cochetti (ed.) 1993.

Rettig, J.
1996 "Beyond 'cool'. Analog models for reviewing digital resources". *Online*, 20, 5, <http://www.onlinemag.net/SeptOL/rettig9.html>.

Revelli, C.
1996 "Problemi di conservazione", I – II, *Biblioteche oggi*, 14, 8: 46-51; 14: 9.

Rossi, P. (ed.)
1990 *La memoria del sapere. Forme di conservazione e strutture organizzative dall'antichità a oggi*, Roma-Bari, Laterza.

Rothenberg, J.
1998 *Avoiding Technological Quicksand: Finding a Viable Technical Foundation for Digital Preservation*. Council for Library and Information Resources, Commission on Preservation and Access, January 1998, <http://www.clir.org/pubs/reports/rothenberg/contents.html>.

Rouse, R.H. & M.A. Rouse
1979 *Preachers, Florilegia and Sermons: Studies on the Manipulus Florum of Thomas of Ireland*, Toronto: s.n.

Samurin, I.E.
1964-1967 *Geschichte der bibliothekarisch -bibliographischen Klassifikation*, 2 v. Leipzig, Veb Bibliographisches Institut.

Santoro, M.
1998 "Biblioteche domani. Il mutamento delle prospettive bibliotecarie all'alba del terzo millennio", *Bollettino AIB*, 38, 3: 303-322,
<http://www.aib.it/aib/boll/1998/98-3-303.htm>.
1999 "Il terminale uomo. I bibliotecari e le nuove tecnologie fra passione e ossessione", in Foglieni (ed.) 1999.

Schneiders, P. & P. Richards
1997 *Some Thoughts on the Function of Library History in the Age of the Virtual Library,* <http://www.ifla.org/VII/rt8/1997/thoughts.htm>.

Serrai, A.
1990 *Conrad Gesner*, Roma, Bulzoni.

1980 "Storia della biblioteca come evoluzione di un'idea e di un sistema", in *Sistemi bibliotecari e meccanismi catalografici*, Roma, Bulzoni: 39-40.
1983 *Guida alla biblioteconomia*, Firenze, Sansoni.
1989 "La storia delle biblioteche: un concetto da riformare" in *Il Bibliotecario*, 22: 187-189
1992 "La 'disciplinarietà' di Storia delle biblioteche", in *Il Bibliotecario*, 33-34: 217-224.
1994 *Biblioteche e bibliografia. Vedemecum disciplinare e professionale*, Roma, Bulzoni.

SMITH, A.
1998 "Preservation in the future tense", *CLIR Issues*, 3, May/June. <http://www.clir.org/pubs/issues/issues03.html#preserve>.
1999 *Why Digitize?* Council for Library and Information Resources, Commission on Preservation and Access, February 1999, <http://www.clir.org/pubs/reports/pub80-smith/pub80.html>.

SOLIMINE, G.
1995 *Controllo bibliografico universale*, Roma, Associazione Italiana Biblioteche.
1998 "Struttura dello spazio e tipologia dei servizi: analisi storica e prospettive della lettura e della consultazione in biblioteca", *Il Bibliotecario*, 15, 2.
1999 *Le raccolte delle biblioteche. Progetto e gestione*, Milano: Editrice Bibliografica.

SPERRY, J.A.
1957 "Egyptian libraries: A survey of the evidence", *Libri*, 7, 2-3. <http://pandora.nla.gov.au/index.html>.

TASK FORCE ON ARCHIVING OF DIGITAL INFORMATION
s.d. *Preserving Digital Information. Report of the Task Force on Archiving of Digital Information*, commissioned by The Commission of Preservation and Access and The Research Library Group.

THOMPSON, J.
1977 *A History of the Principles of Librarianship*, London: Bingley.

THOMPSON, J.W.
1940 *Ancient Libraries*, Berkeley: University of California Press.
1957 *The Medieval Library*, New York: Hafner.

THOMPSON, S.O.
1999 "Printing and library development", in Wiegand &. Davis (eds.) 1999: 509.

TURKLE, S.
1984 *The Second Self. Computers and the Human Spirit*, New York, Simon & Scuster.
1996 *Life on the Screen - Identity in the Age of the Internet*, London, Wiedenfeld & Nicholson.

WEITEMEYER, M.
1956 "Archive and library technique in ancient Mesopotamia", *Libri*, 6, 3.

WELLISCH, H.H.
1999 "Alexandrian Library", in Wiegand & Davis (eds.) 1999.

WIEGAND W.A. &. D.G. DAVIS (EDS.)
1999 *Encyclopedia of Library History*, New York & London: Garland Publishing.

Paolo Ciancarini and Michela Saviane

THE FUTURE OF MEMORY OVER THE INTERNET

We discuss a concept of "collective memory" defined as a set of documents available over a medium like the Internet. We see how such a collective memory accessible over the Internet is effectively shaped by two key technologies, namely languages for describing documents and their structures, and some programs ("search engines") able to classify and trace documents on demand. The future of memory over the Internet will be strongly influenced by the evolution of these technologies.

1. The Internet is a market

When new media appear, it usually takes some time before it becomes clear which uses they will have. For instance, the Internet was invented at the end of the '60s for special military situations, namely to offer during a war a more reliable communication medium than the plain telephone network. Then, during the '70s, some scientists started using it as a research support tool: they used the Internet to exchange ideas, data, programs and scientific documents. Only during this decade did it become clear that the Internet is a new mass medium.

In fact, all specialized sources report that today more and more people visit the Internet. Figure 1 describes an estimate of the distribution of Internet users.

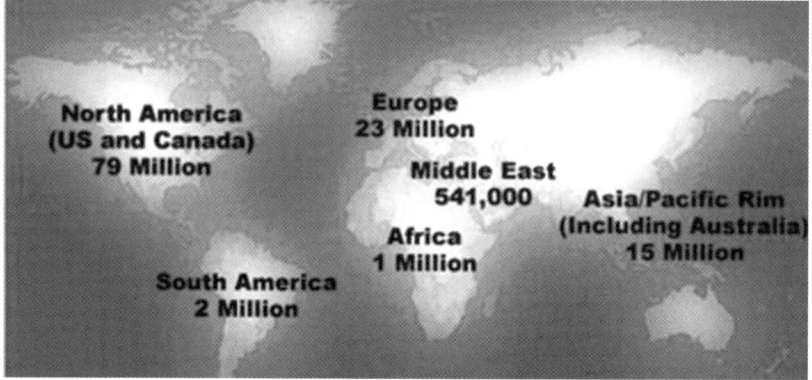

Figure 1. An estimate of the distribution of Internet users in October 1998.

At the end of 1998 Internet users were about 150 millions. The Computer Industry Almanac gave (29 Dec 1998) a prediction which doubles such a figure for the overall Internet population in the year 2000 in the 15 most industrialized countries:

Country	Internet population (in millions)
United States	132.3
Germany	22.9
Japan	21.9
United Kingdom	17.0
France	12.6
Canada	11.6
Italy	10.6

Top 15: 267.5 millions	Europe: 102 millions	*Worldwide*: 327 millions

Figure 2. Estimates on Internet population.

Although the Internet population has a gender distribution that is quite similar to the world distribution (Males: 54% Females: 46%), the distribution of people by age is quite peculiar:

Age group	% online World	% online USA
13-19	14%	41%
20-29	14%	31%
30-39	11%	33%
40-49	10%	30%
50+	5%	22%

Figure 3. Internet population by age.

The table in Figure 3 shows that teenagers are the most devoted Internet user group. This can be explained in at least two ways: teenagers are the most skilled Internet users; teenagers have more time to spend navigating the Internet.

This figure explains also why people who use the Internet for more serious activities are currently a minority: only 10% of users buy goods over the Internet, and only 7% use it for banking.

Companies	25%
Products	25%
Travel	22%
Finances and investments	18%

Figure 4. Users who exploit the Internet to get information on some subjects.

These figures show that the Internet is currently being used as a medium for commerce by a minority of users. However, services like Ebay <www.ebay.com>, which offers personal auctioning so that anyone can sell or buy goods with the utmost simplicity, make us believe that electronic commerce over the Internet will increase and will probably dominate the Internet usage in the near future.

In this paper we intend to discuss the Internet as a medium to build and shape collective memory. More precisely, we discuss a concept of "collective memory" defined as a set of documents available over a communication medium like the Internet. We will see how the collective memory is actually shaped by two key technologies, namely languages for describing documents and their contents, and some programs ("search engines") able to classify and trace documents on demand. The future of memory over the Internet will be strongly influenced by the evolution of these technologies.

This paper includes the following sections: Section 2 describes the Internet as a huge repository for documents; Sect. 3 shows how search engines are currently offering services to "shape the memory" of both single users and whole companies and institutions. Sect. 4 concludes the paper.

2. Has the Internet a memory?

Although some users already perceive and use the Internet as a market, for the moment it is still technically best known as just a set of computers and connections between them, which allow their users to exchange messages. Some computers offer services to store, catalogue, and access information in the form of either documents or databases.

The Internet has been easily available to most researchers in Computer Science since the end of the '70s. However, only after 1995 did it become a major communication medium. In a world already offering several communication media, such as TV, radio, telephones, mail, newspapers, etc., the explosive diffusion of the Internet we have witnessed since 1994 is explained by the fact that people find it more and more useful for supporting commerce and social relationships.

It is important to understand that the Internet not only allows people to communicate, but it also lets them create and access shared information repositories, namely sets of persistent documents. Intrinsic interactivity and persistence of messages are probably the major differences between the Internet and other communication media: newspapers, cinema, radio, TV, the telephone network, the mail system, are all media which can be used interactively and can offer some form of access to an information repository. However, while the Internet offers these functions "for free", because they are part of its core, other media need special (and expensive) structures to enable users to interact or access persistent information.

In this paper, we define an *information repository* as a collection of documents, data, programs, or any combination of them.
Documents and data are represented and stored in several forms:

ASCII, the standard code for representing characters inside an electronic system.

HTML, the standard markup language for documents accessed through the WWW (but a new standard markup, XML, is forthcoming).

Proprietary word processing formats (eg. .doc for MS Word™)

Proprietary printer-oriented formats (eg. Adobe™'s PostScript and PDF).

ASCII is the most ancient (binary) code for representing information inside a computer. HTML is a markup language introduced with the WWW service; XML is a new standard markup language which could substitute HTML in the near future.

Both documents and databases are *persistent*, meaning that they survive the programs (and the people) which create them. Thus, we define as "Internet memory" the set of documents and data available on the Internet via one of its services, for instance the World Wide Web (there are other services, such as, for instance, FTP or Gopher), whose documents are "mostly" HTML documents (there are other document formats, such as, for instance, PostScript or PDF).

It is difficult to evaluate the size of the "Internet memory". If we assume that there are currently say 10^8 computers connected, and each computer contains documents and data for 10^{10} bytes, we have overall 10^{18} bytes, namely one billion of Gigabytes. Note that the size increases each day: for instance, currently (June 1999) in one day Altavista discovers and indexes 250.000 new HTML pages.

This huge size means that it is impossible to browse the Internet memory without any help.

Of course some help comes from the fact that most HTML documents are hypertextual, that is, they are linked to other documents: a user reading a page P can navigate and easily find another related page Q if the author of P included in it some links to Q. Another important issue is that the author of a document can insert in it, apart from the content, some special information about the document itself, which is called *metainformation* and is useful to index or catalogue the document itself.

2.1 What is an electronic document

An *electronic document* is an entity defined by its contents, its internal structure, its relationships with other documents, and one or more "behaviours" (or semantics). Intuitively, any document carries some *information* and has some *structure*: a book, a report, a letter, a program are examples of documents with different formal structures. For instance, a book can be defined by a structure including a title, an author, a publisher, some chapters, a table of contents.

Any document has some physical representation: *e.g.*, writings on paper or drawings on a wall. When documents are stored inside a computer they have a *physical representation* based on some code (e.g. ASCII or UNICODE, a more modern standard) and some *logical structure*. For instance, the logical structure could be given in terms of a tree of headers and paragraphs. In markup languages like HTML the logical structure is determined by using tags which also have some typographical semantics, thus confusing two different concepts.

In fact, when we consider a document abstractly, it is fully defined by its content and logical structure, which is an instance of a *document model*, i.e. an ontology of entities apt to describe text elements (e.g. chapters, sections, paragraphs, pages, etc.). Different people and different programs use different document models, and this is a problem when they have to communicate by exchanging documents. The same document model could be displayed by using different typographical rules. In HTML the two concepts are confused. On the other hand, the new standard markup language XML is able to define the structure of a document independently from its typographical management.

Last but not least, some relationships that a document has with other documents can be represented by a *hypertext superstructure*: for instance, the relationship between a poem and its notes in a commentary could be represented by a hypertext. The hypertext superstructure is an instance of a *hypertext reference model*, that is, an ontology governing the possible relationships between documents. Authors can use different document models and different hypertext reference models, and this fact makes it difficult to construct document catalogues and indexes.

2.2. Operating on electronic documents

When stored and manipulated inside a document manipulation system, a document displays some *behaviours*:

– a *rendering behaviours* defines how a document is displayed on an output device, such as a screen or a printer; for instance, the PostScript™ language is used to describe the rendering behaviours over PostScript™ printers;

– a view, or *control behaviours*, defines how a user can interact with a document (eg. using a hypertext browser); for instance, some HTML tags define how a user can put in some data by filling some fields inside the document and thus obtain an output;

– a *semantics behaviours* defines how the document contents can be analysed with respect to some rules (eg. to see if it is in keeping with some standard); an example is metadata tags, which help search engines to index the document contents.

In general, electronic documents can be *classified* according to their content, structure, or relationship with other documents.

Another important operation on electronic documents is *interchange*, which happens when two different applications (with different internal representations) share the same document (we say that they *interoperate*). The ASCII code has been until now the code most frequently used to represent and thus interchange electronic documents, but it is too primitive for most non-Latin alphabets, so other codes (eg. Unicode) have been defined and are being used.

Moreover, in order to represent the document structure ASCII is useless: an ASCII document is simply a string of characters. Mark-up languages such as SGML, HTML, and now XML (eXtendible Markup Language) have been invented exactly for the purpose of declaring and structuring document types and their instances.

3. The Internet as a collective memory

If we consider the Internet as a very large set of electronic documents, we have to address the following question: how can one access the document(s) that are the most interesting for some specific purpose? In fact, the simple act of storing a document somewhere in the Internet is useless if such a document is not accessible or, more importantly, if it is accessible, but cannot be found when necessary.

Figure 5 is quite interesting because it shows that about 50% of all addresses someone looks into comes from a variety of sources, such as friends or other media, while the other 50% or so comes from search engines.

Links from other sites	17.6%
Algorithmic search engines	17.0%
Ontological search engines	13.1%
Friends	12.7%
Press	12.3%
TV	6.9%
Signatures in E-Mail msgs	5.9%
Books	5.2%
Usenet news	4.6%
Other	4.7%

Figure 5. Sources of Web addresses.

The most important concept in order to retrieve whatever document is *metainformation*: the authors of documents and collections of data also produce "metadata", namely data which describe a document or a data collection and help classify it.

For instance, an author of pages for the WWW has to decide which queries allow him/ her to find his/ her page. In HTML document keywords and descriptions are created with the META tag:

Example:

```
<META    name="description"
   content="a recipe book for chocolate cakes">
<META    name="keywords"
   content="recipe chocolate cake dessert mousse">
```

The importance of metadata cannot be overemphasized; however, in a worldwide environment like the Internet it has a potential problem, well known to all librarians: if no universal standards for metadata exist, as many different classification schemes arise as there are metadata authors.

There are several services which catalogue the available documents, by using either directly their content or their metadata.

All services use one of two methods to classify documents:

- full text indexing, which allows no text to go wasted; however large documents (>50 Kilobytes) are seldom fully indexed;

- selective text indexing, which assumes that the text in a document is not all the same: for instance, its title, first paragraph, and links to other documents are very important.

Today the most popular services to query the Internet memory are *search engines*, which are programs periodically scanning the whole Internet memory in order to copy and classify documents, and to make them available when someone asks them a query.

There are two ways to ask a search engine. The first is by keyword or logical keyword expressions . The basic idea is that who asks has to decide which keyword he/she is interested in and to form a query by using these keywords and some logical operators.

THE FUTURE OF MEMORY OVER THE INTERNET 71

Example (excerpt from Lehnert 1998):
> You ask a search engine:
> I need a chocolate mousse recipe for a dinner party with eight people > you get 50,000 answers
> I need a +chocolate +mousse recipe for a dinner party with eight people > you get 5,000 answers
> +"chocolate mousse" "eight people" "eight servings" "8 people" "8 servings" > you get 1,000 answers
> "chocolate mousse" AND ("eight people" OR "eight servings" OR "8 people" OR "8 servings") > you get 44 answers

In this example the queries are more and more refined: they can differently exploit metadata inside available documents, and get more and more relevant results.

Search engines typically allow us to express refined queries by using the logical boolean expression. However, as a matter of fact, a low percentage of users is able to take advantage of boolean connectors.

AND	5 %
OR	0,2 %
AND NOT	0,2 %
( )	1 %
+	5 %
-	3 %
" "	6 %

Figure 6. Popularity of boolean connectors.

Figure 6 shows the percentage of people interviewed at the GeorgiaTech University in 1998 who declared to use some boolean connectors:

The second way to use a search engine is by browsing categories and subcategories, when a human intelligence has organised available documents into a *directory*. A service based on a directory allows a user to choose a topic and then carry on a deeper and deeper search, until he/ she finds the document he/ she is looking for. Directories often contain the same documents arranged into different categories, which gives the reader more chances to find what he/ she is looking for.

Example:

Let us suppose we are looking for the official site of the British Museum, we can find it by following two different paths:

Regional > Countries > United Kingdom > England > Counties and Regions > Greater London Entertainment and Arts > Museums and Exhibits >British Museum

Regional > Countries > United Kingdom > Society and Culture > Museums and Exhibits > British Museum

Searching by categories is easier than searching by keywords and it often gives more pertinent results; however, in this case we always have to keep in mind that we are dealing with a subjective catalogue: it is useful for us only if we understand its classification schemes.

3.1. A classification of search engines

The most popular search engines have a high commercial value. It is not surprising that these search engines are very dynamical services, because they have to fight competitors to keep their market shares. The most popular search engines are depicted in Figure 7. (Source: GeorgiaTech Univ. 1998).

Yahoo	93,4 %
Altavista	81,4 %
Infoseek	70,2 %
Excite	69,9 %
Lycos	68,2 %
HotBot	46,2 %
WebCrawler	45,6 %
AOL NetFind	20,8 %
Metacrawler	15,1 %

Figure 7. Popularity of search engines in 1998.

Since it is very dynamic and influenced by market forces, the "hit parade of search engines" is not very interesting from a scientific viewpoint. We believe that it is more interesting to study if there are structural differences between search engines. In fact, according to the way they work, we classify search engines in three categories: *syntactic*, *semantic*, and *pragmatic* search engines.

3.1.1. Syntactic search engines

Syntactic search engines are based on programs (robots) which periodically scan the whole WWW, find new or modified pages, and rank them using some formal criteria on their content. The most famous ones are Altavista, Excite, Hotbot, Infoseek, Lycos, and, for Italy, Arianna. They usually have a very huge database. Even if none of them is able to cover all the documents stored in the WWW, their databases are enriched and updated every day.

A syntactic search engine gives a score to any page that uses its keywords, depending on their occurrence and position in the text (for example, a higher score is given to pages which have keywords in the title, the first paragraph, and links to other documents). Then, it answers to keyword queries retrieving documents with the higher scores.

Some syntactic search engines index the special metatags allowed by HTML documents, so that the authors can shape their documents in an ad hoc way to match the formal criteria used by the search engine and to obtain a good score for the most interesting keywords. The activity of "massaging" HTML documents in order to improve their score has a commercial value and is called "Web positioning".

3.1.2. Semantic search engines

Semantic search engines are based on the work of a staff of experts that judge sites with respect to content criteria, select the most interesting ones and classify them into directories of categories and subcategories. The most popular ones are Yahoo!, Looksmart, The Open Directory, and, for Italy, Virgilio. They aim not so much to rank all documents in the WWW as to offer guided tours into the most useful document collections. Semantic search engines exploit both the information included in the document, and the meta-information defined by the authors of the document when they submit their sites. Metainformation includes, for example, a short description, keywords, and the suggestion of a proper category. Nevertheless, the directory staff have the last word to decide if and how to classify the site.

Semantic search engines are used by browsing categories and subcategories, even if they usually offer a simplified interface based on keywords.

3.1.3. Pragmatic search engines

Pragmatic search engines are based on surveys on the behaviour of Internet users at different levels. The most famous pragmatic search engine is Direct Hit, which registers the users' behaviour in front of the list of results retrieved by a common syntactic search engine, like Altavista, to create a new list of results whereby the most visited sites are given the first positions . Another important pragmatic search engine is Google, which registers the usage of web pages according to quotations by other web pages, thus favouring the most quoted ones.

Interestingly, pragmatic search engines, which generally use keywords, are not directly based on the information inside a page but on some metainformation that cannot be controlled by webmasters.

3.2. Shaping a collective memory

Different search engines give different categories of people the power to shape the future of collective memory.

Syntactic search engines give webmasters a real chance of supporting and making their pages popular, as long as some formal rules are followed during the creation of the pages themselves. In fact, a new profession was born: a *Web positioner* is someone who is able to guarantee the positioning of a page among the first 20 or 30 answers, when some questions are asked to a major search engine. The job of a Web positioner is not easy, because the ranking rules of syntactic search engines are not public. Thus, a Web positioner sometimes engages in a virtual fight to improve the ranking of a customer who competes for some market (and of course s/he has to refuse to take other customers interested in the same market). In short, a new, Orwellian, profession was born: a Web positioner is someone able to manipulate results by search engines when someone asks some questions.

Example: You are a novelist, and have just published a new book. You want that when someone asks Altavista for a new novel to buy and read, your own novel appears among the first 10 answers. If you simply advertise your book by putting some texts in your home page, you have no guarantee that Altavista will give a high rank. If you recruit a Web positioner, s/he usually guarantees to position your page among the first 20 or 30 answers when some questions are asked to the major search engines.

How can a Web positioner perform his/her job? What is especially important is that s/he knows how search engines classify the pages they find in the Internet.

AltaVista gives higher priority to keywords that are closer to the top of the page. It gives higher priority to keywords appearing closer to each other in the text page. It adds the occurrences of the keyword in the page for higher scoring. It gives higher priority to keywords in META tags. If there are no META tags used, AltaVista indexes the first 30 words of the page and uses them as the page description.

Excite uses a complex indexing algorithm to determine relevance. Generally, the program attempts to discern the primary "theme" of the page by selecting the sentences for the summary that best reflects the presumed theme of the page.

All search engines periodically re-index the pages they know about, so companies also need to watch their rankings periodically, in order to avoid to be "outranked" by rival companies. Interestingly enough, there are no guarantees: all the search engines change their indexing algorithms from time to time (some search engines modify them weekly).

In order to limit the malicious manipulation of metadata, some syntactic search engines have adopted some defensive behaviours (antispamming): they punish pages with an excessive and malicious use of keywords; they do not trust all metadata; and they often change their ranking rules to be less predictable.

Semantic search engines, on the contrary, put the Internet collective memory in the hands of a limited group of people. They judge with personal criteria both the information in the documents and the metainformation given by webmasters when they submit their sites to be included in the engine catalogue. Since they are mainly operated by humans, semantic search engines are slow both to feed and update, and in general they are not complete, that is, they catalogue only a small subset of the Internet. Moreover, the rankings given to the available pages are always subjective and questionable. This explains why these services are considered centralized and "aristocratic". The possibility has recently been discussed to buy the attention of a semantic search engine about a web address, to speed up its review of the related site. Even if it does not mean buying a site into them, nevertheless this risks leading to an aristocratic, or even worse, "plutocratic" type of collective memory, reserved to an affluent elite of providers.

Finally, pragmatic search engines give a whole community of users the power to build a collective memory , which has the effect of guaranteeing a kind of democracy. Nevertheless, pragmatic search engines tend to become very conservative, because they increase the popularity of already popular sites while sinking unknown sites into oblivion. Thus, after all, they risk narrowing down the collective memory.

3.3. The value of memory: specialized search engines

The Internet memory has a high value, both for profit- and non-profit based enterprises. For research and teaching purposes, the Internet is rapidly substituting real libraries and journals: information on Internet is fresher, easier to use, and more detailed.

The most well-known and used search engines, such as AltaVista and Yahoo!, aim to include all documents of the Web (even if they are destined to keep up with the continuous growth of the Web) or to select all the best sites of the Web. Interestingly enough, most companies managing search engines are supported by advertising: customers search information on products, and the search engines are used to select and choose them.

However, there are several areas in which it is useless to catalogue the whole document base of the Internet. In fact, since profit-based companies rely more and more on the Internet, some important and growing research and commercial areas are using search engines specialized in a specific domain.

Example: NetDetective is a commercial syntactic search engine specialized in personal information. From the NetDetective home page you can:

– Locate e-mails, phone numbers, or people's addresses
– Get a copy of your FBI file. Check driving and criminal records
– Find debtors and locate hidden assets
– Locate old classmates, a missing family member, or a long lost love
– Dig up information on your friends, neighbours, boss
– Discover employment opportunities from around the world

Example: ResearchIndex <http://csindex.com> is a syntactic engine classifying citations *inside* scientific papers on the Internet (at the moment, only a Computer Science document base is active, including 150.000 documents and 3.000.000 citations). ResearchIndex reads the papers and creates a citation index to be used for literature search and evaluation. Compared to traditional citation indexes, it is much more convenient as regards cost, availability, comprehensiveness, efficiency, and timeliness. ResearchIndex computes citation statistics and related documents for all articles cited in the database, not just the indexed ones.

Citation context: ResearchIndex can show the context of citations from a given paper, allowing a researcher to see immediately what other researchers from given papers, and new papers matching a user profile

Related documents: ResearchIndex locates related documents by using citation- and word-based measures, as well as it displays an active and continuously updated bibliography for each document.

Full-text indexing ResearchIndex indexes the full text of the articles and citations.

Personal temporal profile. ResearchIndex computes the personal "productivity" profile in terms of citations/year

Figure 7 page 78 shows (part of) the result of the query about the name "Ciancarini" made by using this service. The picture shows how many times per year this author is quoted inside the document base known to the service. Moreover, the most cited article and the contexts where it is cited are available.

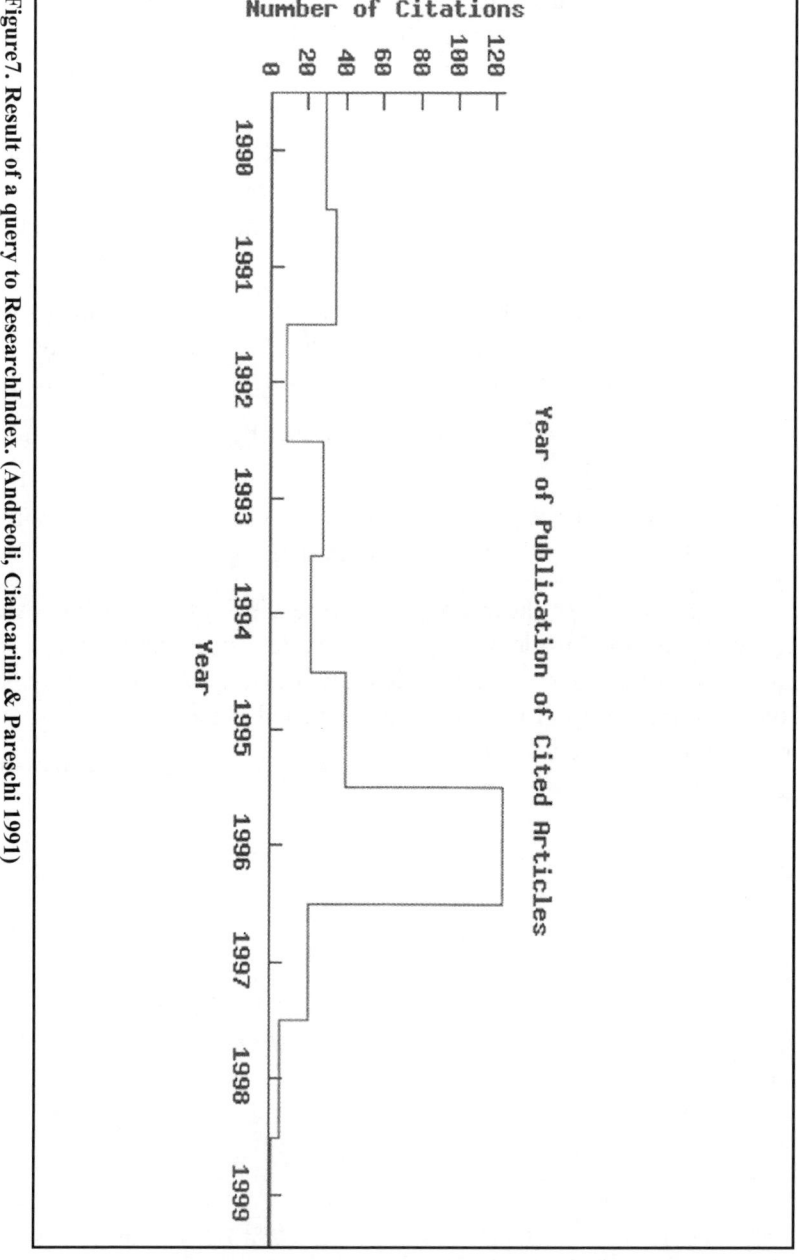

Figure 7. Result of a query to ResearchIndex. (Andreoli, Ciancarini & Pareschi 1991)

4. Conclusions: the future of search engines

People rely more and more on the Internet in order to support their personal and collective memory. The huge number of documents available under the various Internet services makes it difficult for every document to stand out and come to the collective memory, so that the Web positioning has become a real business.

Search engines have a big responsibility in ranking documents and choosing which ones to recall in the collective mind at any query and which ones to leave in the oblivion. Thus, it is important to understand that every search engine has the power to shape the collective memory in different ways.

We can say that, on the one hand, syntactic search engines tend to make memory as big as possible and rely on the users' ability to cope with it and to be familiar with boolean queries.

On the other hand, semantic and pragmatic search engines tend to narrow memoryand help users to manage it.

Semantic and pragmatic search engines are probably more comfortable for users. They promote and extend the use of Internet, even among non-experts or intellectually lazy people,which explains why their use will probably increase in the future.

Anyway, syntactic search engines cannot be replaced as regards the most particular and deeper interests: they will always be preferred by people who are keen on an independent and creative use of the Internet.

Moreover, we foresee that in the next few years the likely replacement of HTML with XML will give another chance to syntactic search engines. In fact, XML will change the basic syntax of Web documents, offering several structuring functions. XML will make it possible to specify meaningful metainformation, by establishing the role of every part of the text in a document. As a consequence, it will be possible to search a keyword among Web documents by specifying its place in a document structure.

Example:

> If you are looking for texts written by Albert Einstein, you can search for "Albert Einstein" among all the <Author> elements of all the XML documents.

Evidently, the condition for such a XML syntactic search engine would be a general agreement on a common set of XML elements.

As a result, syntactic search engines will become more precise and useful, safeguarding the real richness of the future of memory.

Acknowledgements

Thanks to Fabio Vitali for discussions, suggestions, and discoveries.

References

ANDREOLI, J.-M., P. CIANCARINI & R. PARESCHI,
1991 "Interaction abstract machines", in *Proc. of the workshop Research Directions in Concurrent Object Oriented Programming*.

BAEZA-YATES, R. & B. RIBEIRO-NETO
1999 *Modern Information Retrieval*, Addison Wesley Longman Limited.
<http://www.sims.berkeley.edu/~hearst/irbook/>

FAH-CHUN, C.
1996 *Internet Agents-Spiders, Wanderers, Brokers and Bots*, New Riders Publishing.

GILSTER, P.
1996 *Finding it on the Internet*, New York: Wiley.
1997 *The Web Navigator*, New York: Wiley.

LESNICK LESLIE-MOORE, R.
1997 *Agenti di ricerca*, Milano: Mc Graw Hill.

LEHNERT, W.G.
1998 *Internet 101. A Beginner's Guide to the Internet and the WWW*, Addison-Wesley.

On line references

BRIN, S. & L. PAGE
The Anatomy of a Large-Scale Hypertextual Web Search Engine. Proc. 7th Int. WWW Conference, Brisbane, Australia,
<http://www-db.stanford.edu/pub/papers/google.pdf>

COVER, R.
1998 *The SGML/XML Web Page. XML and Semantic Transparency,* last modified November, 24, 1998, <http://www.oasis-open.org/cover/xmlAndSemantic.html>

HARMANDAS, V., M. SANDERSON & M.D. DUNLOP
1997 *Image Retrieval by Hypertext Links.* Proc. SIGIR-97,
   <http://www.dcs.gla.ac.uk/~mark/publications/harmandetal.pdf>

MALTZ, D. & K. EHRLICH
   Pointing the Way: Active Collaborative Filtering. Proc. CHI 95,
   <http://www.acm.org/sigchi/chi95/Electronic/documnts/papers/ke_bdy.htm>

MARCHIORI, M..
1998 *The Quest of Correct Information on the Web: Hyper Search Engines.* Proc. 6th Int. WWW Conference, Santa Clara, USA, 1998,
   <http://www.w3.org/People/Massimo/papers/WWW6>

SEARCH TOOLS CONSULTING & AVI RAPPORT
1998-9 *XML and Search,* <http://www.searchtools.com/info/xml.html>

Search tools

MOTORI DI RICERCA: <http://www.motoridiricerca.com>

TOP30: <http://www.toptrenta.com>

WMTOOLS - WEB MARKETING TOOLS: <http://www.wmtools.com>

SEARCH ENGINE WATCH: <http://www.searchenginewatch.com>

STARS ONLINE: <http://www.stars.com>

Bruce Sterling

THE BIRTH AND DEATH OF MEMORY

Hello, my name is Bruce Sterling, I am a writer and journalist from distant Texas. My speech today concerns "The Birth and Death of Memory".

This part is the birth of my speech. Very soon, I promise you, we will have the death of my speech. In between, I hope to say something memorable.

So, let us begin with the birth of memory. When was memory born? I am a writer, I am not a neurologist. My interest lies in forms of memory that can survive the death of the individual brain. Not memory within consciousness, but memory's lasting traces in the physical world. In other words, symbols. Records. Archives. Language. Media.

Therefore, I re-phrase our question. When was media born? The earliest physical evidence of symbolic records are found in bones. These prehistoric artifacts are prepared sections of animal bone, about the length of one's hand. These bones have grooves cut into them. These are deliberate, intentional, symbolic marks: long, careful rows of parallel cuts.

Microscopic analysis of these cuts shows that they were not made all at once. They were not decorations. They were accounts.

These grooved bones are records. We do not know what they were recording. There have been many speculations, of course. They might be phases of the moon, astronomical records. They might be calendars, records of days passing. Perhaps they are economics: days spent in some kind of labor, or accounts of gifts, or accounts of services.

This is all theory. All we know is that these notched bones are, by far, the longest-lived system of records that the human race ever created. These bones were born about 100,000 years ago, and they died about ten thousand years ago.

This bone technology was very widespread and successful. Notched bones of this type have been found in prehistoric excavations all over the planet. The technology never advanced, and the technology never decayed. The notched bones always looked very similar, no matter where they were found. This practice lasted ninety thousand years.

This much is well-attested. But were these bones were the true birth of media? I fear we underestimate our ancestors. The bones are fossil media, but the fossil record is untrue to the past. Time does not preserve reality: time preserves only what time fails to destroy. The Stone Age left us a lot of evidence in stones, but this does not mean that stones were the core technology of the Stone Age.

If you study the lives of contemporary Stone Age people, you soon come to realize that their world is not made out of stones. Their world is made out of wood, bark, fiber, bone, shell, juices, poisons, toxins, drugs, thorns, hide, leather, string, skin, hair, fruit, seeds, roots, meat, and feathers. These are all organic materials. They rot easily, they decompose, they are very temporary. Time does not preserve them. The very first records created by human beings probably did not survive.

And what were these original physical records? Perhaps we can look to the apes. An American scholar named Susan Savage-Rumbaugh studies the bonobo apes in the African Congo. These chimpanzees live in tribes of about a hundred apes. Every morning, the large tribe breaks up into small family groups, and they go out in the jungle to forage for food. They sometimes use primitive tools, such as the famous chimpanzee termite-stick. Chumpanzees have also been known to use stones as tools.

The small groups of apes separate all day, and they wander over many miles. At night, however, without fail, the small groups always gather together again, into the large tribe. But they do not gather where they started. No, they gather in a different place.

The question then arises: how do the apes know where to go at night? Susan Savage-Rumbaugh says that the answer is simple: the apes mark the trail. Certain trails, you see, are already written into the landscape through the passage of animal bodies. Animal trails are a protomedium, a physical record of intents, and needs, and resources. Even an ant knows that following a trail will lead you to something good and useful. Some animals can track each other through scent, but chimpanzees have a bad sense of smell. So they mark the trail = = they tear up the landscape. They bend and break branches, they tear off big leaves and place them carefully on the ground, to point the way they have gone. The apes that follow read these symbols, and they follow them.

So, these apes leave symbolic messages by deliberately changing the vegetation. Unfortunately for them, they're not very good at it. Bonobo chimpanzees have never gotten beyond the left bank of the

Congo River. The other side of the Congo River is a lovely place, but they have never gone there.

The same might be said for a proto-human stock, the extinct species we call Homo habilis. The Homo habilis species never left the nurturing landscape of Africa. But another extinct species, Homo erectus, exploded out of Africa, and travelled all over the world. Homo erectus crossed rivers, explored over mountain ranges, crossed great plains and deserts.

You might ask how this pre-literate, pre-human group of animals managed this great feat of travel, which no previous ape could perform. Perhaps they were just hardier than other apes. Or perhaps, they knew where they were going.

In Australia, pre-literate humans knew where they were going, because they had a system of marking trails. These were the legendary "song-lines" of Australia, and they were set up in a very deliberate, very poetic fashion. Great chunks of bark would be ripped from trees, leaving huge scars on the tree. Or branches would be stripped of bark and tied together with strips of hide. After a few months, the branches would grow together permanently, creating an artificial, human-made sign in the natural landscape.

With this system of signs came a system of poetry. Children were taught to sing the landscape. When they understood the songlines, they could sing their way from landmark to landmark, over thousands of kilometers.

The passage of time would erase this medium. But it was still a communication system of great power, because it might allow small groups to migrate with purpose and intelligence, to a known destination. Imagine that starvation is on the land, and that you, Homo erectus, know the songlines, but that Homo habilis, your older brother, does not know. Your advantage over him is spectacular; you will survive, he is doomed. Media becomes a matter of evolutionary life and death.

My suspicion, therefore, is that media was born about two and half million years ago. Media is much, much older than the human race.

The thing I like about this media origin theory is its missing link. A marked trail is a missing link between unintentional marks = = the tracks and trails that an animal body leaves naturally, as it moves through the landscape = = and intentional symbols, a sign hacked into a tree, a human sign that is given a mythic, religious, poetic meaning.

We have no record of this theoretical prehuman medium. A marked trail is temporary by its nature, it could not survive the passing of its landscape. But prehistory has many such concepts, mostly unsupported by evidence. We have no record of the entity we call "protolanguage," which is the theoretical state of language between the grunting and gestures of apes, and the human world of syntax and grammar. But we believe in the concept of protolanguage anyway, because it's very hard to believe that human grammar sprang up suddenly out of nothing at all.

In today's world, there is no such thing as a "primitive language". Primitive people have extremely complex languages. The only primitive languages we have belong to brain-damaged people. Or, to the spaces between established languages, the broken world of pidgins and creoles. Even a new-born pidgin, the halting two- word communications of refugees, conquered peoples and prisoners, cannot stay primitive. In a generation at most, it becomes a creole, and in a few generations, it becomes a thriving mongrel vernacular, like English.

The deep past is full of theoretical phantoms. Let us consider the imaginary language "Nostratic", which is said to be the ancestral language stock of the Indo-European family of languages. "Nostratic" is at least ten thousand years old, possibly much older.

Interestingly, the marks of landscape seem to be preserved in Nostratic. Some of its root words seem to be involved with mountains, rivers and rushing streams, the paleolithic world of the south Caucasus and eastern Anatolia. If media arose from attempts to mark the landscape, perhaps the Nostratic language, too, arose from attempts to name the things in one's own immediate surroundings. To name the plants and animals is to know them. To know them, gives you the ability to use them, to survive. So perhaps we can say that languages of the Stone Age rose up from their region, that they grew there, like fine vintage wines.

A human language is a giant memory system, an intricate creation of millions of people, over thousands of years. Every human language has a regional version of reality. Each language cuts reality at some different angle. Even a humble dialect takes a chip from the broken stone of reality.

This brings us to the melancholy topic of the death of memory. Because across the world today, small, local languages are dying. Along with the mass extinctions in the natural world, the postindustrial epoch is bringing us mass extinctions of languages. It is difficult to quantify what we are losing by this, but we are definitely losing something of importance. People cheerfully die for the sake of their native language. When a language has died, what have we lost? Some vital aspect of the memory of a people.

My own native language is English, which is the great, globalized language primarily responsible for crushing all the other languages. English crushes those languages under its feet, like grapes in a global tub.

I know this is true. I admit it to you. I feel all the pain one feels at a sad event which causes one to benefit very much. I am an author of English-language books, so every death of a small language suggests more readers for me. I would point put, however, that the noble Italian language is also far from guiltless in this regard.

Let me refer you to the very interesting and extremely morbid "UNESCO Red Book of Endangered Languages". There are hundreds of dying languages around the world, so we will concentrate on Europe. UNESCO's Red Book numbers 94 languages on the European continent. Europe has forty-three Indo-European languages, twenty-five Finno-Ugrian languages, six Turkic languages, plus Kalmyk, Cypriot Arabic, Basque, Romani, seven Jewish creoles, and nine diaspora dialects. Fifty of these 94 European languages, more than half of them, are considered endangered languages by UNESCO.

Since I speak in the ancient and honored Republic of San Marino, I must point out that the local language, "Emiliano Romagnolo," is one of those endangered languages. Italy is crammed with endangered languages. They are all being crushed like grapes by the televised Italian broadcasts of great media businessmen, like your former Prime Minister.

It presents a great moral difficulty for an English speaker like myself to even publicly recite the names of these victim languages. My Italian accent is so horrible that it will probably make this list of victim languages sound unintentionally comic. But despite all this, as a gesture of respect, just to show that I am paying attention, let me publicly recite the names of: Cimbrian, Algherese Catalan, Provencal, Ladin, Friulian, Molise Croatian, Gallerese Sardinian, and the native tongue of San Marino, "Emiliano Romagnolo". English is not killing these languages. Italian is killing them. The mighty Italian language, the unifying force of a Group of Seven advanced industrial nation.

I am not a linguist. I prefer engineering to syntax. If you looked at the paper I distributed to accompany this lecture, you will see that I am an amateur historian of media technology. My interest in the subject of the death of memory came about through studying new media.

Many of us here at this "Future of Memory" conference are deeply involved with new media, with historical databases, the social impact of television, digital libraries, information agents, and so forth. The reason I myself am among you is that I discovered that no one was keeping track of the new media that *did not work*. Everyone in the industry of creating new media wants to promote and sell new media, but most new media *do not work*. They fail and they die. They do not become the next dominant medium. New media do not carry civilization forward in safety, handing the torch the culture to the next generation. On the contrary, they mostly become dead media. Any memory entrusted to the care of these dead media becomes a dead memory.

The Internet in particular, the great titan of new media, is a fiendishly efficient device for destroying local languages, and local heritage, and local memory. Broadcast television was also very good at this. I give television every credit for enforcing national character, and destroying local character. I have seen this happen in my own region: the effect of national American television on regional cultures like Acadian Louisiana and the Texas-Mexican border has been absolutely astonishing. These backward, impoverished areas were almost obliterated by television in a single generation.

But the Internet is even more powerful, because it encourages the user to talk back and take part. Television merely floods the landscape from a central source, like a kind of paint. People under television are the oppressed; people on the Internet are collaborators. The Internet appears at the user's fingertips, and seductively asks him to take part in the global world, to become a global citizen.

A global citizen has very little time or motivation to learn preindustrial regional languages. In my own case, these languages would be Comanche, Tonkawa and Lipan Apache. Comanche, Tonkawa and Lipan Apache are the languages spoken two hundred years ago in my home town of Austin, Texas. I am sure these languages have many valuable pieces of data about how to skin bison, dig roots, and live off the land of Texas in huts made of leather. I can guarantee you that I have no intention whatsoever of learning to speak these languages. UNESCO cannot make me learn them. A moral crisis cannot make me learn them. I bluntly refuse to learn them. I am far, far too busy surfing the Internet.

Why? Because the Internet sends electronic mail inviting me to go to conferences in distant San Marino. Mastery of Comanche, Tonkawa, and Lipan Apache will never give me these valuable things. I do not defy the global Net. No, I choose to be here with you. By that very choice, I carry a message of doom.

For the third part of my speech, let me turn to the subject of archival memory, or the collected history of the human race. Why do archives die? There are many possible causes.

First, entropy. The passage of time. Natural decay. The elements. Insects. Fungus. Fire. Flood. Earthquake. Undergraduates. Paper can last for centuries if it is well cared for, but it can also turn to mush in a matter of hours.

Second, mnemonicide, or the deliberate killing of memory. Human malice. This happened to the Mayans when their libraries were burned. It happened to the Incas when their knotted strings were burned. It happened in China at the command of the first Emperor. It happened under Stalin in the Soviet Union. It is happening in the Balkans today.

The third reason is obsolescence. Indifference. Loss of interest. Civilization does not break down, there may be no foreign invaders, but the media of one's ancestors goes out of vogue. The archives are no longer seen as possessing any value. Cultures change. People lived under the stone monuments of Egypt for hundreds of years with no idea how to read them. The Babylonians built their homes out of broken cuneiform bricks, the clay records and accounts of the past.

One recalls the legendary words of doom: if these books deviate from the Koran then they are blasphemous; if they agree with the Koran, then they are superfluous. In the contemporary epoch this might be rephrased: If it's on the Net then we have it already, and if it's off the Net, then obviously nobody wants it.

Digital data is easy to reproduce, but it still has no archival format. There is no permanent way to store digital data. This is a great and terrifying scandal. There are problems in the hardware, problems in the coding schemes, problems in the formats.

It would be a simple matter for our civilization to create digital archives of tremendous, unparalleled scope: if we had the money and the political will. We have money. We have no political will. My great fear for the "future of memory" is that history will become part of the culture industry. Culture as we have understood it since the Renaissance could dissolve into the stream of media, like salt in water. All memories will be for sale. Any memory without a commercial value will not be supported or sustained.

This is a nightmare vision, but nightmares can be useful things. One imagines a version of Orwell's 1984 where Winston Smith is not a political ideologue, but a software salesman. No return on investment? Into the memory hole.

What does this nightmare look like in detail? It looks like this. Our heritage is no longer the heritage of mankind, but a commercial part of the heritage business. An old castle is no longer an old castle, but a painted simulacrum for the tourist trade. Universities become non-governmental organizations, or, even scarier, post-governmental organizations. We no longer sympathize with the thinking of the past, but merely try to retail its commercially attractive aspects. Memory becomes a commodity. Cultural identity becomes a consumer choice. Bad archives are deliberately favored by the market, because they are the culture-industry's version of planned obsolescence. A computer that swiftly breaks and decays can be sold to us again. We will buy the same music again and again, in different formats, on tape, vinyl, CD and DVD.

In this media-saturated world, the archives of the twentieth century might still be visible, like scratch marks on old bone. But the motivation behind them would be lost, no longer understood. There would be no past and no future, just the flow of data and the rise and fall of the market. In that imaginary society, in that dystopia of commodity totalitarianism, the media of liberal democracy would have no meaning. Just as we ourselves see no meaning in the long-lost media devices of Athenian democracy, such as the kleroterion, the ostraka, and the clepsydra.

Would history end? No. History does not end. But speeches must end. This speech has ended. Thank you for your attention.

Fabio Vitali

ON THE DURATION OF RICH DOCUMENTS

1. Introduction

When you reach the top of the stairs you are in a huge room several stories tall. It is dimly lit from a slot cut through the living rock of the mountain on the southern face. [...] You are able to show the dial around [a] sphere, now showing you the year in the cryptic method of keeping time when this clock was built. It reads the year 11.567. [...] You are struck that the people of this ancient time had the foresight to think this far into their future and create this place.
At this point you wonder through the rest of the facility to find a library and people accessing and preserving the data stored there. Akin to the truly ancient library of Alexandria, there is a constant forward migration of the data to increasingly better and denser methods of storage. In the main vault you find the original 1.000 books stored at the impossibly large scale of 100 nanometer pixels. These were the first 1.000 books stored in the Clock/Library chosen by its founders. Although not necessarily relevant to your time, what they began helped to teach people the value of knowledge over long periods of time. Without it humanity might have obsolesced itself out of existence without being able to look over the ancient records of the sea and air and find trends that are only apparent over centuries or millennia (Brand 1999).

In these years straddling between two centuries, two millennia, possibly two civilizations a gigantic, fascinating, and heroic engineering project is being designed and organized: the long-term project to build a large mechanical clock, powered by seasonal temperature changes, in order to provide fuel and meaning to all thoughts overcoming the pathologically short attention span that characterises our times. As the computer designer Daniel Hillis proposed in 1995:

When I was a child, people used to talk about what would happen by the year 2000. Now, thirty years later, they still talk about what will happen by the year 2000. The future has been shrinking by one year per year for my entire life. I think it is time for us to start a long-term project that gets people thinking past the mental barrier of the Millennium. I would like to propose a large (think Stonehenge) mechanical clock, powered by seasonal temperature changes. It ticks once a year, bongs every once a century, and the cuckoo comes out every millennium.

The project is symbolic in its conception, shape, and intended effect: a stable, reliable, and long term construction of a big and impressive slow clock, aimed at inducing thoughts of long term projects, endeavours, and responsibilities. Along with the Clock, a huge Library will be built to store permanently (or as permanently as we can now imagine) and incrementally all the texts and data that have long-term relevance, significance, and effect. The purpose is to dilate the concept we have had so far of the Now, which has shrunk enormously into just a few generations, and to put our current action in the right perspective to produce effects in the future.

The *Clock of the Long Now*, as the project is called, and the Library associated to it, constitute an important signal of the growing interest in the long-term management of our culture. Major and influential personalities are part of the leading committee, such as Esther Dyson, Paul Saffo, Mitchell Kapor, etc. Further information about the project can be found in the relative Web site, <http://www.longnow.org>, and in Brand (1999).

How would one design such library? Would it be digital or printed? How much information should be put in it? What is the physical medium that can presumably store a quantity of information over a foreseen life span of ten thousand years? Printed with ink on acid-free paper? Or stored on magnetic tape? What data format can we use that could last ten thousand years? Roman letters drawn with black ink on acid-free paper? ASCII text? HTML? Microsoft Word?

Even information that can last a century would still constitute an unreachable goal. We can hardly make paper sheets that last a hundred year, or digital media that last a few dozen years. The digital world allows, indeed, to copy information rapidly and safely from old media onto new media, but this requires constant awareness, attention and care, because digital media, when they fail, fail utterly and definitely. A loss of a few bytes in some critical positions of a disk (in the boot sector, for example) may render several gigabytes of data completely unreachable.

But even shorter, it seems, is the life span of data formats: although we can obtain a perfect copy, byte by byte, of a WordStar or a WritePerfect document that was written fifteen years ago, we will most probably not be able to open it with any word processor, although those applications were among the best selling applications of the time.

The problem worsens for graphic formats, and even more for custom-built applications.

The real problem with data formats is that for several years the persistent representation of data on disks has been considered a by product of the activation of the corresponding computer programs: document files were meant to be created with the same application that would later be used to display them, modify them, and print them. Since applications often need to be updated, are not ported to new hardware architectures or new operating systems, accessing legacy files may become a problem. The first years after the demise of a popular application, most new applications will probably include a converter from the old format into the new one. But rapidly these options are felt useless, unnecessary, hard to maintain by the programmers, and are soon discarded from subsequent releases.

If a file format depends on the application that can write and read it, then the life expectancy of the file format is identical to that of the application itself. But if the data format is not strictly connected with the application, then the two life spans become independent, and we can hope to get subsequent, innovative applications that can read and write the same data format.

Standards are good for this: new applications appear every month, but good standards take years in creating, and have much longer life expectancies. GIF and JPEG, both formats for graphics and images, were not designed to work with any specific application, but , over several years, several generations of independently created applications have been programmed to handle pictures stored in these formats.

The XML language, like its predecessors SGML, was created for documents that have to last. The emphasis on describing the semantics of the data, rather than the functionality that needs to be activated with it, makes SGML and XML documents independent of these functionalities, and flexible to undergo both old and new applications without changes.

But even though obsolescing data formats may be won by standard and semantically rich data formats, the problem of preserving data is even more complicated. Virtual documents created dynamically by complex applications on the Internet make the very object of preservation a fuzzy and evanescent concept. It is unclear whether we can and should preserve any single output of these applications, or whether we should try to preserve the very engine that can create these outputs.

What of ongoing drafts, ever-changing documents that never reach a final, preservable form? What of chats, portals, weblogs, and all those Internet live documents whose form can have neither a printed form nor a content persisting in time?

As usual, solving a problem changes the very problem. Electronic information has been difficult to preserve, to migrate to newer hardware and software architectures, to access even after a few years after it was created. The Internet and the World Wide Web have brought forth the idea of a network of everlasting documents that are easy to access, to mirror, to backup and restore. Yet, the shameful confusion created by abusing HTML, by forcing into our Web documents those meagre graphical effects that HTML could provide, already shortens the useful life of our documents considerably. Even worse than that: due to specific and intrinsic reasons, dynamic virtual documents cannot have a preservable state. Thus, how can we preserve them?

But first things first. We had better start by examining the issue of long-term preservation of computer data, and determine if there are classes of documents that will be intrinsically difficult to preserve. Then we should concentrate on XML as a specific solution to the preservation of a large class of document types, besides being a very good idea for many other aspects of document management. Only finally will we contemplate the preservation problems of dynamic and virtual documents on the Internet.

2. What are we preserving, anyway?

Consider this paper, a simple computer file created with one of the most popular word processing applications of one of the most popular operating systems on the market . In order to know how to preserve it, we need to understand how the paper ends up in bits, currents and magnetic fields on the media we choose to use.

The words that make up this paper are stored according to a specific *character encoding*, which transforms the letters of the alphabet into bit patterns. The word processing application decides the encoding based on the operating system and the human language of the document.

The word processing application provides numerous functionalities for formatting, which would allow me, were I interested, to paginate the paper with a sophisticated layout and typographical effects. In fact, I don't really care for such a formatting, since the paper will be handled by a professional editor that will override the formatting instructions that I might have selected and will provide a consistent appearance and style to all the papers of the same publication. Still, the word processor adds – albeit simple – information about the formatting options that I have selected and stores it with the words that make up the paper. Thus the actual file is composed of both my words and the commands of the word processing application. The designers of the program decided that these two types of information would be mixed up in order to maximize the efficiency of the application, and thus what the program writes on disk is a complex and unreadable mass of characters within which my words are difficult, if not impossible, to sort out.

The application does not directly access the physical media on which the document will eventually be stored, but instructs the operating system to do so for it. The operating system receives the document as a data block, and, completely ignoring the content, encoding and format of the document, it wraps it with some additional information useful for cataloguing and retrieval: a user-decided name, an access path, the current date and time, the name or identifier of the application itself. Lower levels of the operating system, at the file system level, may well decide to cut the data in fixed-size chunks that optimise the storage on the media, and provide means to reconstruct the original data from all the pieces.

The operating system, though, does not directly control the storage medium, but relies on an additional piece of software, that is, the driver of the peripheral. This driver knows the details of the unit it is controlling, what commands it can perform, in what order the commands should be given, and what to do in case of one of several dozen of error types.

The unit finally receives the commands from the driver and performs the actions requested, transforming the different data it receives into minuscule magnetic fields, electric currents of minuscule electronic circuits, reflection properties of minuscule areas of the media surface, etc. The document is finally stored in a persistent manner on a physical medium.

As we have seen, there are several independent layers of software and hardware activities between my words and my disk:

character encodings
(to convert letters of an alphabet into a predetermined bit pattern);
data formats
(mixing content – my words – and application functions – formatting properties of the document – in the same data entity);
operating systems
(providing information about my data – metainformation – and splitting parameters for archival and retrieval efficiency);
hardware drivers
(providing support for the actual operations of the unit);
hardware units
(performing the operations intended to persistently activate the medium to store the data).

In order to design the preservation of documents such as a paper, we have to consider all these aspects in all their ramifications.

The most evident characteristic of these aspects is their volatility. Continuously and frequently, all these aspects evolve, change and outdate older choices: new applications, or new versions of the same application, are made available that add different types of data to the content, new operating systems handle files and meta-information differently, new drivers need to be loaded to exploit newer functions of our old and new hardware, and even the character encoding is not stable, but new encodings are coming out to provide support for more alphabets, for documents in multiple languages, etc.

Usually, of course, new software and hardware provide support, or at least upgrade paths, for older generations than themselves, but this support rarely spans backward for more than one or two generations: a distraction of a few years is enough not to allow some data to be read with newer computing set-ups.

Fortunately, with minimum care, we can overcome most of the problems caused by evolving hardware, drivers, and operating systems; as noted in TFADI (1996), there are now ways to handle unavailability of hardware and software platforms. *Migration of data* on newer media or operating systems provides a longer life to our data. Fortunately, copying comes at a continuously lower cost, since newer media usually cost orders of magnitude less than older ones, and computers are orders of magnitude faster that those of previous generations. Thus we can easily estimate that, even though we will keep on accumulating more and more data on devices that in time will become obsolete, it will become easier and cheaper to copy them on newer devices.

Furthermore, the availability of large, inexpensive hard disks and wide area networks may further improve our future in this regard. The habit of using tapes for long-term storage of copious quantities of data is disappearing, and huge databases for public use are now frequently put on line, on hard disks of networked computers. While our recent past presents us with many situations whereby old, off-line tapes become unreadable in time (as noted in TFADI 1996 again, the 1960 American Census data were recovered incompletely and with incredible effort, and the 1970 satellite observations of the Amazon basin are now completely lost), we can safely assume that migration of data, or at least network backups, are now becoming a routine task whenever newer hardware is being installed. It is well known that disk space is growing at a greater speed that our ability to fill it (Lesk 1999), and analogously for the time needed to copy it.

Nonetheless, these somewhat reassuring thoughts do not apply to the more evanescent aspect of obsolescence: data formats. What will we do if our perfectly preserved huge quantities of data can only be read by an application that became outdated years ago, and is now incompatible with the current generation of operating systems?

Sometimes, the applications themselves are what is deemed worthy of preservation. For instance, video games (Babich 2000) have peculiar characteristics with respect to other types of applications: games usually depend entirely on the hardware architecture they were designed for, and thus badly migrate to newer systems, even when these claim full compatibility with old ones. Furthermore, games are usually important not so much for the documents they can produce as for themselves, the activity they perform, and the entertainment value they give their users. The best way to preserve these artifacts is through the emulation of the hardware platform they used to run on. The retrogaming community therefore has chosen to produce emulators to make obsolete games available on current generation computers. For instance, the MAME project aims at producing emulators for most of the arcade game computers produced in the eighties. Similar projects exist to emulate old home and game computers, such as the Commodore 64, the Apple II, the Nintendo Gameboy, the Spectrum ZX, etc.

Most of the times, anyway, it is not applications that we want to preserve, but the documents have produced with them. Preservation or emulation of the original hardware platform on which the applications used to run is a sub-optimal solution, as Steve De Rose notes (1999):

> Why would I want software and data doomed forever to run only on the machine it started on? Typically, it would run much better – not just faster – on newer devices. In many cases, the original target hardware is barely capable of running software anyway, given programs' tendency to expand to fill the space and power available to them. […] If one encapsulates everything, new technologies cannot be applied. What if I want to use the data in a new way? A slavish adherence to the limitations of old media is often passed off as if it were the virtue of preserving the strengths of those same old media. […] Thus systems often slavishly emulate [old media's] weaknesses, or even more commonly forget to support the electronic medium's compensating strengths.

As we see it, the preservation of data is not simply a matter of survival of computer bytes across time, but rather it is a way to rephrase all the organizational aspects of the production of these bytes.

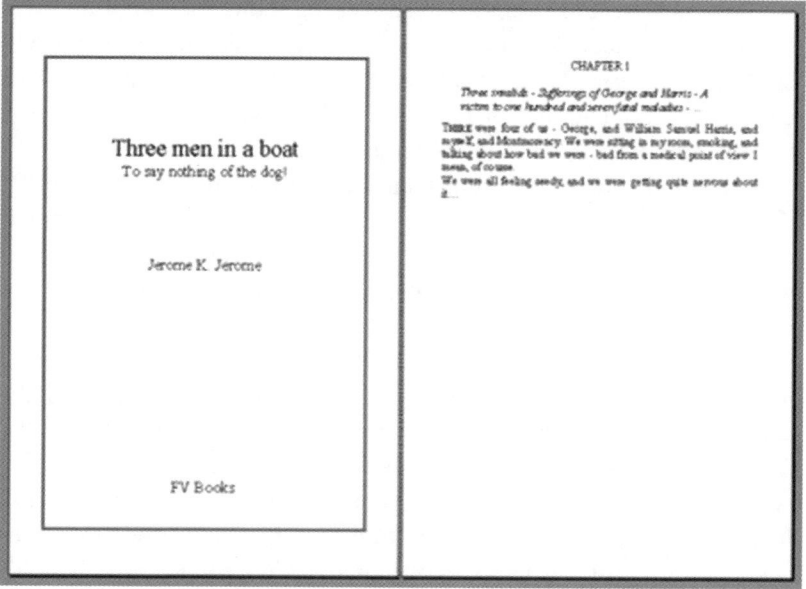

Figure 1. A very simple MS Word example.

We have to understand that a computer document is not important just for the tasks we perceive important when we create it, but that in time new uses may arise for these data that we could not foresee when we created them. If we organize the production of our data so as to allow new, unforeseen uses of them, we cannot just preserve our documents, but extend their useful lifetime.

The data format is a key factor in this organizational restructuring. Leaving the decisions on the data format to the application designers is simply unacceptable: the many economical and technical constraints would lead them to choose just the data format that is easiest to implement. These data formats may have three main problems:

> They may be **binary**, that is, a plain dump of the data as it is stored in memory by the application. In binary data there is no discernible structure in the data, and only the original application has the necessary knowledge to determine, by virtue of the position alone, the role and meaning of each chunk of data. This makes the data format hard to interpret in absence of the original application, and the data themselves provide no hint of how it should be read.

> They may be **proprietary**, that is, a format whose details are decided by the application designers only. These formats are not often given to the public, and even if they are, in any moment they are usually subject to any modification the owners decide to do. Only the owners have a solid chance, and often the commercial interest, to provide software that reads and writes this format.

> They are **application-oriented**, that is, they contain direct references to specific functions; every application provides a set of functions that can be executed by users to manipulate their data. Usually these functions add information to the data: they may specify that some text is to be shown in bold, or that some part of an image has a special color palette, etc. The added information, which we will call markup, usually reflect directly the functions of the application, and cannot be preserved without the original application.

Most application data formats are binary, proprietary and application-oriented. In order to clarify the properties of these kinds of format, I will provide here a simple example, using MS Word as the source application. In fact, having many of the above mentioned characteristics, MS Word can write documents in a variety of formats.

The simple document we will consider is the beginning of a novel as it could be prepared by a publishing house. In figure 1 I show the result on screen using the MS Word application.

MS Word allows its documents to be saved in several formats. The standard format is a binary format (the so-called ".doc" format), which is shown in figure 2.

Figure 2. The binary format of a MS Word document.

There is little of immediately understandable in the binary format of Word: the document as stored on disk contains most of the information elements in a manner that can only be interpreted by an application. Some of the text can be discerned, but it is impossible to understand, at a glance, the role and meaning of the majority of the content of the file.

MS Word also provides the possibility to save the document in an equivalent, non-binary format, called RTF (Rich Text Format). While ".doc" files may contain any kind of character, RTF files only use printable characters, and clearly differentiate content from application commands. Thus RTF files can be laboriously read by humans without the aid of specialized applications. Nonetheless RTF is clearly a proprietary format: each new version of Word modifies and expands the grammar of RTF, and forces other applications to update their RTF filters to keep up with the innovations. Each expansion adds new terms to the RTF vocabulary, making it quite difficult to understand the exact meaning of every command. Figure 3 shows the RTF version of document shown previously.

```
{\rtf1\mac\ansicpg10000\uc1
\deff0\deflang1040\deflangfe1040{\upr{\fonttbl{\f0\fnil\fcharset256\fprq2{\*\panose 02020603050405020304} Times New Roman;}{\f4\fnil\fcharset256\fprq2{\*\panose 02000500000000000000} Times;}
}{\*\ud{\fonttbl{\f0\fnil\fcharset256\fprq2{\*\panose 02020603050405020304} Times New Roman;}{\f4\fnil\fcharset256\fprq2{\*\panose 02000500000000000000} Times;}}}}{\colortbl;\red0\green0\blue0;\red0\green0\blue255;\red0\green255\blue255;
\red0\green255\blue0;\red255\green0\blue255;\red255\green0\blue0;\red255\green255\blue0;\red255\green255\blue255;\red0\green0\blue128;\red0\green128\blue128;\red0\green128\blue0;\red128\green0\blue128;\red128\green0\blue0;\red128\green128\blue0;
\red128\green128\blue128;\red192\green192\blue192;}{\stylesheet{\widctlpar\adjustright
\lang1033\loch\af4\hich\af4\dbch\f4\cgrid \snext0 Normal;}{\*\cs10 \additive Default Paragraph Font;}}{\info{\title }{\author Fabio}{\operator Fabio}
{\creatim\yr2000\mo4\dy9\hr17\min36}{\revtim\yr2000\mo4\dy9\hr17\min36}{\version2}{\edmins0}{\nofpages3}{\nofwords72}{\nofchars412}{\nofcharsws505}{\vern117}}\paperw11906\paperh16838\margl1134\margr1134\margt1417\margb1134
\facingp\deftab708\widowctrl\ftnbj\aenddoc\hyphhotz283\margmirror\formshade\viewkind1\viewscale100\pgbrdrhead\pgbrdrfoot
\fet0\sectd
\linex0\headery709\footery709\colsx709\endnhere\sectdefaultcl
{\*\pnseclvl1\pnucrm\pnstart1\pnindent720\pnhang{\pntxta .}}{\*\pnseclvl2\pnucltr\pnstart1\pnindent720\pnhang{\pntxta .}}{\*\pnseclvl3\pndec\pnstart1\pnindent720\pnhang{\pntxta .}}{\*\pnseclvl4\pnlcltr\pnstart1\pnindent720\pnhang{\pntxta
```

```
)}}{\*\pnseclvl5\pndec\pnstart1\pnindent720\pnhang{\pntxtb
(}{\pntxta )}}
{\*\pnseclvl6\pnlcltr\pnstart1\pnindent720\pnhang{\pntxtb
(}{\pntxta
)}}{\*\pnseclvl7\pnlcrm\pnstart1\pnindent720\pnhang{\pntxtb
(}{\pntxta
)}}{\*\pnseclvl8\pnlcltr\pnstart1\pnindent720\pnhang{\pntxtb
(}{\pntxta )}}{\*\pnseclvl9
\pnlcrm\pnstart1\pnindent720\pnhang{\pntxtb (}{\pntxta
)}}\pard\plain \qc\widctlpar\brdrt\brdrtnthsg\brdrw45\brsp20
\brdrl\brdrtnthsg\brdrw45\brsp80
\brdrb\brdrtnthsg\brdrw45\brsp20
\brdrr\brdrtnthsg\brdrw45\brsp80 \adjustright
\lang1033\loch\af4\hich\af4\dbch\f4\cgrid {\page
\par \par }{\fs72 \par
\par \hich\af0\dbch\af4\loch\f0 Three men in a boat
\par }{\fs48 \hich\af0\dbch\af4\loch\f0 To say nothing of the
dog!
\par \par \par \par \par \hich\af0\dbch\af4\loch\f0 Jerome K.
Jerome
\par \par \par \par \par \par \par \par \par \par
\par \hich\af0\dbch\af4\loch\f0 FV Books \par }{\fs20 \par \par
\par
\par }\pard \qc\sl-20\slmult0\widctlpar\adjustright {\caps\fs34
\page
\par }\pard \qc\widctlpar\adjustright {\caps\fs34
\hich\af0\dbch\af4\loch\f0
Chapter 1
\par }\pard \li567\ri851\sb400\sa240\widctlpar\adjustright
{\i\fs36 \hich\af0\dbch\af4\loch\f0 \hich\f0 Three invalids -
Sufferings of George and Harris - A victim to one hundred and
seven fatal maladies - \u8230\'c9\loch\f0
\par }\pard \qj\widctlpar\adjustright {\fs34
\hich\af0\dbch\af4\loch\f0 T}{\scaps\fs34
\hich\af0\dbch\af4\loch\f0 here}{\fs34
\hich\af0\dbch\af4\loch\f0  were four of us - George, and
Willia\hich\af0\dbch\af4\loch\f0
```

```
m Samuel Harris, and myself, and Montmorency. We were sitting
in my room, smoking, and talking about how bad we were - bad
from a medical point of view I mean, of course.
\par \hich\af0\dbch\af4\loch\f0 \hich\f0 We were all feeling
seedy, and we were getting quite nervous about it\u8230\'c9
\par }\pard \widctlpar\adjustright {\fs34 \par }}
```

Figure 3. The RTF format of the same document.

Another format that MS Word can save documents in is HTML: this is the standard language for hypertext documents available on the World Wide Web. HTML, derived from SGML and close relative to XML, is not proprietary, but an international standard: a proper body (the World Wide Web Committee, or W3C) manages the development and evolution of the language, and there exist hundreds of applications that can manage this format. Thus HTML avoids the drawbacks of binary formats by being text-based (and thus it is easily readable), and the drawbacks of proprietary formats by being an international standard (and thus it has a controlled evolution and a large base of supporting software).

```
<HTML>
  <HEAD>
     <META HTTP-EQUIV="Content-Type" CONTENT="text/html; char-
set=iso-8859-1">
    <META NAME="Generator" CONTENT="Microsoft Word 98">
    <TITLE>Three men in a boat</TITLE>
  </HEAD>
  <BODY>
     <P ALIGN="CENTER"> </P>
     <FONT SIZE="7">
        <P ALIGN="CENTER">Three men in a boat</P>
     </FONT>
     <FONT SIZE="6">
        <P ALIGN="CENTER">To say nothing of the dog!</P>
        <P ALIGN="CENTER"> </P>
        <P ALIGN="CENTER">Jerome K. Jerome</P>
        <P ALIGN="CENTER"> </P>
        <P ALIGN="CENTER">FV Books</P>
     </FONT>
```

```
<P ALIGN="CENTER"> </P>
    <FONT SIZE="5">
      <P ALIGN="CENTER">Chapter 1</P>
    </FONT>
    <DIR><DIR>
       <FONT SIZE="5"><I>
              <P>Three invalids - Sufferings of George and Harris -
           A victim to one hundred and seven fatal maladies - ... </P>
         </I></FONT>
    </DIR></DIR>
    <FONT SIZE="5">
      <P ALIGN="JUSTIFY">There were four of us - George, and William Samuel
         Harris, and myself, and Montmorency. We were sitting in my room,
           smoking, and talking about how bad we were - bad from a medical
             point of view I mean, of course. </P>
      <P ALIGN="JUSTIFY">We were all feeling seedy, and we were getting
           quite nervous about it...</P>
    </FONT>
  </BODY>
</HTML>
```

Figure 4. A semiautomatic HTML version of the Word document.

Nonetheless, HTML is an application-oriented format: the commands that are present in a HTML file provide specific formatting instructions that are useful for on-screen visualization, but provide no support for more sophisticated uses. For instance, the HTML document shown in figure 4 contains information about the requested alignment of the paragraphs and the font size of the text, but nothing informs us that the string "Jerome K. Jerome" refers to the novel's author, that the content is divided into chapters, or that the sentence "Three invalids - Sufferings of George and Harris - A victim to one hundred and seven fatal maladies - ..." is composed of several items summing up the topics contained in the chapter. Applications different from on-screen browsers will find it hard to draw useful information from this document: for instance, indexing applications will not be able to determine the author or the content or the elements of the chapter summaries.

In this brief roundup, we have shown that text-based formats have advantages over binary formats in terms of clearness and understandability, and that standard formats have advantages over proprietary formats as regards availability and stability. We have further described the disadvantages of application-oriented formats, that inhibit the creation of applications providing additional sophisticated functionalities over existing data. This has an evident impact on the preservability of such documents: most HTML documents, for instance, are optimised for displaying on colour screens of a given resolution that are now widely available. In a few years, we may require these documents to be displayed on the smaller screens of cellular phones, or are read by a synthesized voice in a car-radio system for drivers. Both these applications will make little use of instructions detailing alignment or font size, and will rather require a different class of specifications. Therefore, in just a few years fixing the content of our documents with HTML tags will seriously impede the preservation of our documents. In the next section we will examine how these problems can be avoided with a text-based, standard, data-oriented format: XML.

3. What is XML for?

In a sense, XML (Extensible Markup Language - *sic*!) can be seen as the ultimate answer to our quest for preservable data formats. XML (Bray, Paoli & Sperberg-McQueen 1998) provides a solution to all the issues raised in the previous section, and has many more advantages than those connected with preservation. Its generality, sophistication, and the widespread industry support contribute to make XML one of the most interesting products of computer science.

The most interesting aspect of XML for the purposes of our discussion is that XML is not a data format in the sense that I have been meaning so far: that is, it is not a specific dictionary of terms (words, commands, or bytes) wrapping the content and providing processable information about the content itself. Rather, XML is a meta-format, a common syntax to create and express any dictionary of terms concerning the content of our documents.

XML looks like HTML, and can be easily mistaken for it. Although there are a few syntactical differences, they both use tags, attributes, and entities variously structured and nested to label the important elements of a document. But while HTML is a predefined and closed set of tags and entities, which our documents must be suited to, XML is a way to create any set of tags and entities, so that we can create and customize them for the particular characteristics of our documents. More simply, XML is an HTML where I am allowed to decide the tag names. This apparently simple difference has a great impact on our ideas about marking up documents.

To describe XML and one could simply resort to a fast overview of its syntactical characteristics: XML provides an HTML-like syntax for document elements where the actual names are not predefined but can be decided at will. That is to say, XML maintains the peculiar look of tags, attributes and entities made famous by HTML, but it also allows us to use any name for these tags, attributes and entities. Because of this, even HTML names can be considered valid XML names, so that the following can be considered a "correct" chunk of information in both XML and HTML:

```
<P align="right">This is a correct document element</P>
```

Syntactically, XML is more rigorous than HTML, requiring strict nesting of tags, fully quoted attribute values and proper endings of document elements (ending tags are not optional in XML as they are in many cases in HTML). Nonetheless, many HTML documents are already or can be easily transformed into correct XML documents. Indeed, the HTML document in figure 4 is already a correct XML document (but had to be corrected by hand from the one created automatically by MS Word).

But it is in its ideology that XML mostly differs from HTML. XML brings forth the idea of generic markup, a radically different approach to document markup. The possibility of deciding the names for tags, attributes and entities means that the author has an additional degree of freedom in the creation of documents, and that he/she can tailor the markup of our documents to any needs. Indeed, he/she can tailor it to *all* needs. Generic markup, in fact, insists that markup should not be added with a specific application in mind (say, printing), but that it should describe the document generically, i.e., it should describe the document for what it is rather than for what it is used for.

For instance, it is a mere accident for a block of text within a document to be formatted with a given font or a given margin width, or even to be a paragraph. But sections, chapters, titles, captions, etc. will always remain such, regardless of the style transformation they will be subject to. Figure 5 shows a possible generic markup for our document using the XML syntax.

```
<?xml version="1.0"?>
<!DOCTYPE NOVEL SYSTEM "novel.dtd">
<NOVEL>
  <FRONT_MATTER>
    <TITLE>Three men in a boat</TITLE>
    <SUBTITLE>To say nothing of the dog!</SUBTITLE>
    <AUTHOR>Jerome K. Jerome</AUTHOR>
    <PUBLISHER>FV Books</PUBLISHER>
  </FRONT_MATTER>
  <CONTENT>
    <CHAPTER>
      <TITLE>Chapter 1</TITLE>
      <SUMMARY>
        <ITEM>Three invalids</ITEM>
        <ITEM>Sufferings of George and Harris</ITEM>
        <ITEM>A victim to one hundred and seven fatal maladies</ITEM>
          ...
      </SUMMARY>
      <BODY>
          <PARA>There were four of us - George, and William Samuel
            Harris, and myself, and Montmorency. We were sitting in my room,
            smoking, and talking about how bad we were - bad from a medical
            point of view I mean, of course. </PARA>
          <PARA>We were all feeling seedy, and we were getting quite nervous
            about it ... </PARA>
      </BODY>
```

```
        </CHAPTER>
        <CHAPTER>
           ...
        </CHAPTER>
    </CONTENT>
</NOVEL>
```

Fig. 5. One of the possible XML versions of the document.

While maintaining several similarities with HTML (particularly the use of tags and attributes), it is clear that the XML version of the document pays no attention to layout and typographical issues, but rather it tends to describe the intrinsic structure of the document: where HTML has lots of FONT tags and ALIGN attributes, which are only useful for graphical rendering, the XML version uses tags like CHAPTER, TITLE, etc., i.e., it provides a structural classification of the parts of the document. As discussed in the previous section, XML exhibits all the good characteristics of long-lasting data formats:

> XML is **standard**: it is not proposed by a commercial enterprise but by an organization of standards, the World Wide Web Committee, and it has been widely accepted by hundreds of different organizations.

> XML is **text-based**: it allows the visual exploration of the internals of a stored document even in the absence of the specific application that created it.

> XML is **data-oriented** rather than application-oriented. The ideology behind XML asks the markup to describe facts about the document rather than the application that was meant to manage it.

These aspects cooperate to arouse realistic expectations of preservability of XML documents: it is reasonable to expect at least some of these hundreds of organizations to keep on supporting the format for a long time; it is reasonable to expect, in a far future when specialized applications have vanished, to be able at least to read the documents with a generic tool and to tell the markup from the content. It is reasonable to expect that we will still be able to understand the purpose and meaning of the markup, and therefore to create tools that will let us re-use the content in a meaningful way.

4. Virtual documents

The World Wide Web has taken off as a mass medium with a speed unprecedented throughout history. Most of the organizations with a content or image to be presented to the big public have already opened a site and made their data available. Both as information system for its internal purposes (the Intranet), and as advertisement or customer support system for the users at large, every commercial organization of some size (and many of no size at all), have created on-line shops, manuals, and portals. The Internet is the place where image, support and sales converge to create a unique customer experience.

The Web already holds more data than the Library of Congress. Soon it will hold more stuff than the sum of all the collections of data in the world (Lesk 1999). It will soon become an ordinary, obvious fact for some information to be on the Web, , while the decision to put it elsewhere apart from the Web will be just an option whose advantages and drawbacks will be explicitly considered.

Even if most people consider the Internet little more than an amusement, and most of the commercial organizations see it little more than a advertising opportunity, there are huge quantities of data that are worth preserving out there. Yet the very rapid development of the Internet will create several problems when the question of preserving this huge amount of data arises. One of the most common experiences of the early Web users was the infamous "404 Not found" error, labelling a link as a dead end, and the resource as no longer available. Several initiatives have started looking for a solution to this.

The easiest case may be that the information has just moved. A restyling of the site, and an updating of the available information and its URL are no longer valid. That is to say, the document is still out there somewhere, but the address I wrote down has changed. In fact, the URL contains several local information (for instance path and filename) that may change without warning. The URN initiative (Sollins.& Masinter 1994) plans to provide resources with stable and reliable network addresses . The only way to do so is to plan a resource name that has no bearing with its physical accessing mechanism (domain name, directory, filename, etc.), and to provide a way to map the name according to the current URL. We would then store in our bookmarks and in our links the stable URN, and whenever we need to activate it, the browser would request the current specific URL and access the resource.

Sometimes, on the other hand, the resource just disappears. In 1994 Netscape Communicator decided to introduce a scripting language for HTML pages, and at the beginning of 1995 a big quantity of documents, manuals and white papers appeared on its site to lure programmers and web designers into using the Livescript language. More or less in the same period, the sudden and huge success of Java (which started as a completely independent initiative from Sun Microsystem) led Netscape marketing managers to rename the scripting language. All documents about Livescript were changed overnight, and Javascript became the scripting language of Netscape. No technical change was made, just a renaming. Yet, no mention of the name "Livescript" was left on the site, with a complete rewriting of the past, at least on the site of Netscape. Many similar events have happened on the Web. When an organization is in complete control of the diffusion of the data it makes available, it is very easy to rewrite it to suit the strategies of the moment.

The idea of archiving the data in spite of the owner's approval is tempting. Brewster Kahle's Internet Archive <http://www.archive.org> is based on this idea (Kahle 1997). An automatic process (a robot) systematically requests every page available on the Web; and systematically stores it on a local disk. Every time a stored page changes, the robot asks for the new version, and stores it beside the older ones. The purpose of this section of my paper is to explain why, in my view, this task, however tantalizing it may seem, is intrinsically doomed.

Of course, given the amount of information that is routinely put on the web, this task appears to be gigantic. But it is my conviction that, even if provided with enough resources (disk, computing power, etc.), this task is intrinsically impossible. The main reason for this are *virtual documents* (Milosavljevic, Vitali, & Watters 1999).

I have already mentioned that text-based data formats are extremely interesting for the variety of applications that they allow. Virtual documents were previously unheard of, but thanks to HTML they have become extremely common. In this context, a virtual document may be defined as a document whose persistent state is different from its perceived state. For instance, a view on a database (say, the output of a query) is a document that doesn't exist as such but is built on demand as the output of the query. The content of the document, in this case, is less important than the query that generated it. Another example is a compound document that is built from different chunks of data immediately before being displayed to the user, or a document that is built by an application as its output. The most evident cases are portals, dynamic collections of information chunks, links and services. Figure 6 shows an example of a virtual document.

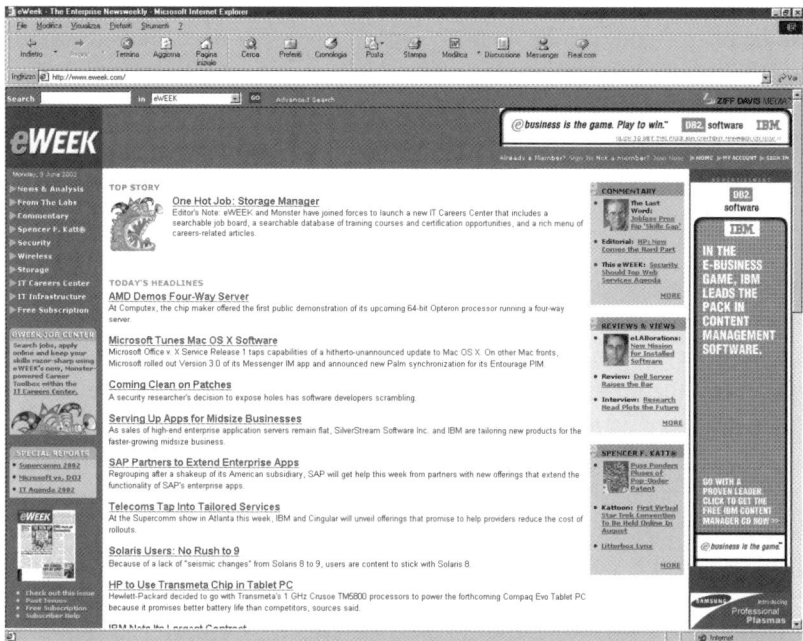

Fig. 6. An example of a virtual document.

In all these cases, the important fact is that the user sees "less than" the real document. He only gets the result, not the machinery to compile the result. The document received by the browser in figure 6, for instance, is not stored in this form anywhere on the original server. In fact, as it often happens, the document is built on demand as soon as it is requested.

Thanks to HTML and its text-based format, it is very easy for an application to format its output so that it is immediately accessible on the Web. Usually an empty HTML template contains just the main structure of the page, with predefined slots for the actual content. When requesting the document, a server-side engine collects the content from a database and applies it to the template to generate on the fly the final document sent to the user.

Preserving the final result is pointless. The analogy to magazines and newspapers does not hold: even though the newspapers are compound documents resulting from intense copy-and-paste activities on the part of those who create it, a newspaper still has a fixed content and regular issuing periods which can be relied on for archival. A web virtual document, on the other hand, can be updated several times per hour, indeed continuously, and in many cases, it is tailored to the preferences and interests of the person requesting it. Furthermore, random processes can be added to let each access differ from the previous ones, thereby enhancing the sense of novelty and the appeal of the site. Therefore, it is no use storing the document as received on the browser, since in a few minutes the same document could very well have a considerably different content, depending on the user requesting it, the amount of new information meanwhile added, or even the random result of a dice throw.

In order to archive a traditional database, it would make no sense to express all the possible queries and store the result. The database is usually considered as a whole and archived as such. Likewise, it makes no sense whatsoever to archive the pages that are generated by a process such as the one just described. It is necessary to have access to the actual text database, to the HTML templates, and even to the actual engine that creates the perceived documents. Only by archiving these three actors correctly can we safely assume we are preserving such a site for the future.

And, of course, archiving the database and the rest of the data cannot be done unless the owners of the data cooperate. The intent to archive the Internet without the collaboration of the actual owners of the datais, therefore, futile.

5. Conclusions

This paper does not end with a hopeful note: the problem of preserving digital documents is not easy to solve. Although we may have learnt from our past mistakes, technology advances and creates new challenges that cannot be tackled with old approaches.

Although XML and its cohort of languages can provide important advancements in the correct labeling and structuring of information, the current trend in Web technologies seems to favor complex, dynamic collections of information that are impossible to define and to archive.

It is hard to say how we should manage, and, frankly, even *whether* we should. Preserving data meant to be consumed fresh may well be considered an unacceptable imposition on the will of the authors of the data. Currently, the cooperation of the owner of the sites is necessary to the preservation of complex data, especially virtual, dynamic documents. It is possible that this is just fair, that the owners should decide whether and what should be preserved and what should be destined to oblivion.

Acknowledgement

I wish to thank Paolo Ciancarini, Giulio Blasi, Dino Buzzetti, Andrea Angiolini and Andrea Babich for the interesting discussions on electronic preservation that led me to write this paper. Giulio Blasi deserves additional thanks for the impressive conference he organized on this topic, "The future of memory" (San Marino, May 1999), and for the patience he has shown in waiting for my contribution. And many, many thanks go to Isabella, who has encouraged me to write this paper.

References

BABICH, A.
2000 *Retrogaming, un caso di digital preservation dei videogiochi*, Master Thesis, Communication Sciences, University of Bologna (in Italian).

BRAND, S.
1991 *The Clock of the Long Now, Time and Responsibility*, Basic Books.

BRAY, T., J. PAOLI & C.M. SPERBERG-MCQUEEN
1998 *Extensible Markup Language, (XML) 1.0*, W3C Recommendation 10 February 1998, <http://www.w3.org/TR/REC-xml>

DE ROSE, S.
1999 *Where did my Bytes go?*
<http://www.stg.brown.edu/~sjd/mymusings/datasurvival.html>

KAHLE, B.
1997 *Preserving the Internet*, Scientific American, March 1997,
<http://www.sciam.com/0397issue/0397kahle.html>

LESK, M.
1999 *How much information is there in the world?*, Time & Bits Conference,
<http://www.longnow.org/10klibrary/TimeBitsDisc/ksg.html>

MILOSAVLJEVIC, M., F. VITALI & C. WATTERS
1999 *Proceedings of the Workshop on Virtual Documents, Hypertext Functionalities and the Web*, VIII Int. World Wide Web Conference, Toronto, Canada.
<http://www.cs.unibo.it/~fabio/VD99/>

MULTIPLE ARCADE MACHINE EMULATOR (MAME)
<http://www.mame.net >

SOLLINS, K. & L. MASINTER
1998 *Functional Requirements for Uniform Resource Names, RFC 1737, Internet Engineering Task Force* (IETF), December 1994
<http://www.ietf.org/rfc/rfc1737.txt>

TASK FORCE ON ARCHIVING OF DIGITAL INFORMATION
1996 *Preserving Digital Information*, a report commissioned by the Commission on Preservation and Access and the Research Libraries Group,
<http://www.rlg.org/ArchTF/tfadi.index.htm>

Andrea Babich

RETROGAMING: FOR A DIGITAL
PRESERVATION OF VIDEOGAMES

1. Introduction

Retrogaming is a trend that has settled among videogamers since the early Nineties. At that time, it was simply meant as the act of playing/enjoying videogames from the past, instead of the most recent ones; by the end of the decade, it became something really complex, a very serious game with thousands of people trying hard to preserve the memory of interactive entertainment. The key factors which allowed the metamorphosis of the purposes of retrogaming are two: the Internet and computer emulation. This essay investigates on how retrogamers learned to use these two instruments together, surprisingly finding out some techniques and ways of interaction which may serve as an example for the whole digital preservation research field.

1.1. Making up for wasted time (more wasted time?)

First of all, let us try to understand why retrogaming was brought to life, and why it did not continue to be just a peculiar playing practice for nostalgic people.

By the Nineties, the 8-bit CPUs, on which classics such as Pacman (1980), Space Invaders (1978) or Donkey Kong (1981) used to run, was no more the state-of-the-art in videogaming technology. 16-bit processors brought graphics and sound to a new level of detail, while new storage formats allowed programmers to grant their games a more complex structure. Anyway, here comes the problem: many videogamers decided that this evolution did not satisfy them for at least three reasons.

Some of them thought that the 16-bit generation of videogames was not revolutionary enough – while sound and graphics were improving, the gameplay lying beneath them was just about the same. So, why bother buying Amiga games when the Commodore 64 would do?

Some other players, while agreeing on the fact that gameplay was evolving together with graphics and sound, found that the increasing gaming complexity was just in antithesis with their own idea of videogaming. The pure arcade action of the Eighties' consoles and coin-ops was dying, together with another great genre of computer game: the text adventure.

It has to be said that in the beginning those die-hard fanatics of retrogaming were a minority among videogamers. Anyway, things were going to change dramatically with the release of Sony Playstation, as well as with the introduction of other powerful gaming technologies which allowed the player to move in realistic 3D environments – a new perspective, a new way of videogaming which redefined the meaning of everything that had been conceived before. The same day new games took the limelight of the gaming culture, old games began to be seriously worshipped, and the cult soon became all but esoteric.

By the mid-Nineties, many software houses smelt a chance of making money thanks to retrogaming. They took the old classics and reprogrammed them for the modern consoles or computers, so that they could preserve all the look-and-feel of the originals without any graphical or sound enhancement: otherwise they would have produced a remake and missed the "retro audience" target.

The business was and still is successful. The "Namco Museum" collections for Sony Playstation, featuring milestones such as Pac-Man, Dig Dug, and Pole Position sold very well both in Japan and in the West; Microsoft's "Return Of the Arcade" for PC and Mac is among the ten top-selling titles of the Nineties.

If this had been the only way retrogamers had for living the classic gaming experience again, they would have settled for that – but they were quite unhappy for several reasons. First of all, the reprogrammed classics were not the original ones, but only well done clones – by the way, the new program code could not mimic the old one to perfection, and most retrogamers know the behaviour of the original game better than their programmers. Secondly, while the purpose of the software houses was to reprogram only the most popular games, retrogamers were often looking for rare, unpopular, underground games, those flawed, dusted-down gems that industry had forgotten, despite their intriguing originality. Thirdly, commercial retrogaming was a somewhat individual experience: an instrument which lets you remember past things, without offering you the chance of sharing them with other people who may feel just the same as you. And some memories need to be shared in order to become a source of strength rather than weakness.

1.2. Beyond the clone culture: Emulation

It has been stated that reprogramming is not what true retrogamers look for, because there exists a better programming technique, whereby the issue is to reproduce the behaviour of a pre-existing games machine flawlessly: it is what we call the *software emulation*. This technique makes a computer or a console able to run applications and games that were meant for some other systems?, even if the emulating system was not originally supposed to run programs from the emulated one. For example, a PC, a Mac or a Playstation 2 can potentially run games from an Atari VCS console, a Commodore 64 computer, a Space Invaders coin-op and so on.

To make software emulation work, two main conditions are required:

– A *program*, the so-called emulator, which translates the contents of the emulated videogame from its original language into that of the emulating system. Emulators 'fool' the emulated videogame, making it believe it is running on its original hardware, while this hardware is only a software illusion, created by the emulator itself, which stores inside its core the set of instructions? of the emulated CPU.

– *Software* to run. It is necessary to copy all the data of the original game from the storage medium of the emulated system to the emulating one, in a format suitable to the latter. The transfer from one system to the other is often called "dumping". Once we have the file/s transferred onto our HD/CD/DVD, we can ask the emulator to run the desired game, as a word processor would load a text document. Depending on the original storage medium, the files brought on the emulating system are appropriately called ROM- or disk- images. Since the emulator works as a translator, it is theoretically possible to make it run every single game from the original system. For instance, an Atari VCS 2600 emulator shall let you play more than 500 games, while all these cartridge images would fill just some megabytes on your storage medium. Regretfully, in order to get a better income, even those commercial products which use emulation instead of reprogramming often gather together only few titles on each volume. Anyway, emulation became retrogamers' favourite practice for another reason, as it will be pointed out shortly.

– *Speed* is a crucial issue, too. While every system can potentially emulate another, for gaming purposes the chipset of the emulation system must be more powerful than the emulating one: translation processes occur in real time, and they take a lot of computational power. Too busy a CPU will steal some power from the routines of video (and sound) rendering, either causing a general slowdown of the screen update ("slow motion effect"), which will drop down below the canonical sixty frames per second, or making the display skip some of the frames to keep the correct emulation speed, losing, nevertheless, a choppy visual experience. It is clear that emulating speed can dramatically change the meaning of a video-match played under emulation: a slow computer will never achieve a visual impact similar to the emulated system, even if it is using data coming from the latter. As a matter of fact, a Pentium II class processor is powerful enough to emulate most of the gaming systems from the Eighties – so/ speed is nowadays a crucial factor nobody seems to worry about, at least when the task is to emulate a 8 or 16 bit CPU.

1.3. A place for (retro)games

Another important factor which made the link between retrogaming and emulation stronger is the way the Internet has been used. Every single communicative protocol of the Internet medium has been colonized by old games' fans, who have created a true "virtual community" through the years.

First of all, the Internet had (and still has) the leading role in making emulation the daily bread for retrogamers. While some emulators are commercial programs, most of them are home brewn applications, created by programmers as a hobby in their spare time, and shared on the Net for free. Everyone can download an emulator and make it run on his/her computer, and this is generally legal, since the emulator itself does not contain portions of the videogames code – it is just an interpreter, created by a reverse engineering technique which does not infringe any copyright. Saying that emulation is "free" does not simply mean that one does not have to pay for it. Amateur programmers often use the Net to cooperate with one another, allowing the free distribution of the source code, so that everyone else can submit a program enhancement, a bug report or some information about the correct behaviour of the emulated system. Both programmers and users are involved: every retrogamer is a potential beta tester, so that, in a way, emulators get better and better thanks to the whole retrogaming community.

As it has already been mentioned, an emulator without the original game images is quite pointless. Since images are nothing but files, they can be put on the Net and shared, too, just like emulators. On the Net, several sharing strategies can be applied/chosen: games and emulators can be stored in HTTP sites or in FTP archives, as well as posted on newsgroups or sent via e-mail. Basically, the whole thing is similar to the MP3 phenomenon, which allows people to download entire CD-quality songs; just as in the mp3 case, downloading game images is illegal, since it violates the most common copyright rules established by the international Berne Convention. Again, like mp3 sites, game archives on the Net have a very short life because of the legal issue, but it is impossible for the copyright owners to monitor the whole Web constantly, since new game sites are continuously popping up. New applications, like Napster or GNUtella, allow users to share files in a more discreet way, which is even harder to detect since they use the Net as a mere transfer medium rather than as a content viewer.

The Retrogamers' notion of "sharing" goes far beyond software files and programming techniques, since one of their greatest needs is to share words, thoughts, and memories. Here we go back to the most common functions of the Web as we all know it, that is, a medium which lets people express themselves via homepages, newsgroups, message boards, relay chat systems and so on. Anyway, the sharing of ideas and that of software must not be seen as two separate worlds: they are merged together in a unique universe of meaning. Such a virtual community, even if originated from the need of reviving "dead videogame media", is, nonetheless, very alive, and all its members are very active in fostering the evolution of the community. One of the most amazing aspects is that opinion leaders of this society are highly aware of the importance of some really serious issues, and keep trying to spread the word about them. Among these issues, there has always been the need for strict rules to preserve games and memories, with a view to reduce the natural hypertextual chaos of the Net. Now, we are going to look at some of the most interesting aspects of this digital preservation effort.

2. Videogames as a digital object to preserve

2.1. Beyond nostalgia

When retrogaming began to acquire visibility on the Net, some critics argued that it was not going to become a big thing – after all, it was a niche project involving a cathartical ritual to defeat the negative effects of growing up in a hostile gaming era. Anyway, retrogaming soon defined itself as an ever-changing reality, evolving both in quality and in quantity.

As far as quantity is concerned, anyone can now download *thousands* of games from the Seventies/Eighties/Nineties; during the last few years even the rarest and weirdest titles have been dumped and released on the Net, ready to be downloaded and played; one can find images of Japanese games never released in the West, alpha prototypes and so on. Since the download is free, and the chances of being caught in such a criminal act are very low, many people grab (or "leech", as the retro jargon goes) every single game they find. One does not download only the games which he/she used to play as a young boy/girl: one starts a *collecting practice*, a bulimic attitude known among retrogamers as "ROM Hunting", since it involves a constant exploring through the meanders of the Internet. The fun is no longer focused on playing the old games, but rather on collecting them all.

As regards quality, we refer to the usually excellent quality achieved by emulators in reproducing old game systems, as well as the new ones, since Sony Playstation, Game Boy Color and Nintendo 64 emulators are also available on the Net. These consoles are still on the shelves and sell strong, so we cannot really talk of ancient game systems: the retro- prefix loses its meaning. Once again, critics said that this was the end of retrogaming, since emulators were now able to run the newest titles and therefore no one would have been interested in emulating older systems. They were wrong again: emulation shifted the interest of retrogamers from the games themselves to the act of collecting, archiving, sorting, finding documentation, and *preserving* them from oblivion. It could sound a bit paradoxical, but to collect a ROM image from Nintendo Entertainment System (1983) and one from Nintendo 64 (1996) is quite the same practice, when the task (and the joy) is to preserve it from the flowing of time; nevertheless, the preservation of older games is a priority, since the risk of losing info or content about them is arguably higher than the one affecting latest titles.

This part of the essay describes the techniques and strategies which the retrogaming community uses in the practice of preserving videogames. To go through our description, we shall make use of the typology enucleated by a fundamental document, "Preserving Digital Information", written in 1996 by the Task Force on Archiving Digital Information. This text suggests possible cures for the several problems afflicting digital preservation in general, but it is very interesting to highlight that many of the solutions proposed by the TFADI are the same ones retrogamers choose in their restricted preservation field. Anyway, videogames are very complex multimedia digital documents, so that their maintenance involves several peculiar questions, which prove useful to reflect upon the status of multimedia documents preservation at large.

The chapter "Information objects in the digital landscape" from the TFADI document is crucial for our work, since it introduces the concept of *integrity*:

> The processes of preserving digital information will vary significantly with the different kinds of objects – textual, numeric, image, video, sound, multimedia, simulation and so on – being preserved. (...) Whatever preservation method is applied, however, the central goal must be to preserve information integrity; that is, to define and preserve those features of an information object that distinguish it as a whole and singular work. In the digital environment, the features that determine information integrity and deserve special attention for archival purposes include the following: content, fixity, reference, provenance, and context. (TFADI 1996)

Videogames are "multimedia monsters" since they present bits from several kinds of digital objects. Even if we agree that emulation is the most faithful way of using old software on new systems, we are just halfway through the process – we have overcome the hardware incompatibility problem, but we still need to concentrate our preserving efforts on the game software as an *object in the digital landscape*. We shall concentrate on the notion of content, fixity and reference, the other ones being less interesting from a strictly technical point of view (even if it has to be specified that retrogamers are really aware of the importance of provenance and context).

2.2. Content: bit stream and beyond

The very first problem one has to face in preserving videogames is to make the emulating system read the binary content coming from the emulated one correctly (from now on, we shall consider the PC as the emulating system). The problem concerns the game bit stream, which needs to migrate from the storage medium of one system to another one. There are two techniques, depending on the type of storage medium used by the emulated system:

– *Connecting the old peripheral to the emulating system.* This technique requires an interface to connect the old system's storage medium (for example a Commodore 64 tape recorder) to one of the ports of our modern system (ie the serial or the parallel ones); a transfer software (downloadable from the Net) will monitor the bit passage. Unfortunately, such connecting interfaces are not sold in shops, but they are home-made by amateurs. It is important to remember that native PC peripherals are useless for this purpose of transferring, even when they look similar to those of the emulated system: for example, a PC 5' 1/4" floppy drive formats disks in a completely different way from a Commodore 64 floppy drive, even if the latter uses the same 5'1/4 floppies.

– *ROM dumping.* Most of past gaming systems use ROM cartridges to store game data, so they have not real peripherals to load games: cartridges act like memory expansions, directly plugged onto the hardware board of the system. Old arcade games work in a similar way, with ROMs soldered to the motherboard. In such cases, it is necessary to build a whole new peripheral to interface the ROMs to the PC port. While a console cartridge reader can be generally used for most of the games created for that system, arcade ROMs often require a special copier for a single game (even if coin-ops also have some kind of slot standards). ROM encryption systems, introduced by manufacturers for anti-piracy purposes, often cause further problems to dumpers, who, nevertheless, help each other to communicate via the Internet until the hacking is done.

Another aspect of the content integrity concerns all the non-digital components of the videogame, which nonetheless contribute to give sense to the game experience. Many consoles and coin-ops used infrared guns, steering wheels and even stranger game controls to involve the player deeply in the gaming experience. The first black and white games used colourful plastic screen overlays. Low quality TV screens used to blur images of your favourite computer game in a peculiar way which cannot be easily reproduced by your 21" Triniton monitor, so that, paradoxically, what you see seems to be even more "pixelated" than 15 years ago. Even worse than that, some classics like *Pong* worked on an analogue platform made of discrete circuits, not digital chips:

> *Pong* doesn't have a microprocessor or code ROMs like most games do. Pong is completely built from discrete electronic components which work together to create the behaviour of the game (...). Since there is no processor we cannot "emulate" Pong in the traditional way. (Boris 1999)

The "emulation plus game images" technique shows its limits when we come to the analogue content of games. Worst of it all, some classics work on a completely analogue "hardware": While some of these problems cannot be avoided (for ex. game controls), in some cases an affordable solution is *simulation*, which is something different from reprogramming:

> In this approach the programmer would write a generic electronic circuit simulation program. He would then input into the simulator the spec of each component in the circuit as well as how they are interconnected and the program would simulate the operation of the circuit in real time and display the results on the computer's screen. (Boris 1999)

2.3. The knowledge of content

Expanding our notion of content, we have to face another problem, as stressed by TFADI:

> Digital archives define content in a way that transcends the limits of the hardware and software systems needed for reading and interpreting the bits of an information object and for rendering it for use in a specific format and structural representation; that is, they define content in terms of *the knowledge of ideas the object contains*. (TFADI 1996)

Let's suppose that we have a fully working game image, as well as a fully working emulator. Can we say we have full access to the game content? No, unless we are able to explore the whole game, from the beginning to the end. This is not a "text linearity vs. non-linearity" problem: even non-linear texts can usually be fully explored by further re-reads. Videogames introduce a peculiar exploring variable: skill. If you are not good at it, a videogame will not let you go that far, and playing the initial stages of a game is not a good way to understand its global meaning.

However, the retrogaming era offers several ways of overcoming the lack of videogaming skill. These ways involve various degrees of cheating, made possible by the emulation/internet fruition frame:

– The Net as a knowledge tool: a web page can store lots of information which may aid troubled players in their quest. The range goes from scans of the instruction booklet to complete walkthroughs of the game posted in text format. Hints, passwords, tips and secrets can be posted as well. The playing of several adventure games can highly benefit from all this side information.

– Game images can be easily hacked and modified, and *trainers* can be inserted as well, so that you can play with infinite amno, energy or lives. This cheating technique is very opinable since it violates the game integrity (see the paragraph 2.4.).

– To move cheaters and trainers from the image to the emulator. Several emulators come with powerful debugging functions, and sometimes with a "cheat search engine", which allows the player to temporarily modify some of the game's parameters, and this works for every game the emulator can run, while the integrity of the image is not violated. Many emulators come with a "save state system", too, so that a player can take a snapshot of his/her progress and post it on the Internet – one can download someone else's match, sit back and enjoy looking at game stages he has never been able to reach.

2.4. Fixity: another dark side of piracy

According to TFADI, fixity stands for the inalterability of a digital document. The less the fixity of an object is, the more chances it will have to go through voluntary or involuntary modifications in its life span. For example, it would be easy for a game dumper to hide his/her written name inside the bit stream, as stressed by TFADI: "on the digital landscape, it is relatively easy for a creator to alter or retract previously released information" (TFADI 1996)

A true retrogamer would never do such a horrible thing, but here we come to another problem – the source of game images. The images are often made from old pirate carts, disks or tapes, so the fixity of the game is corrupted at the root of the transferring process, and nothing can be done except for looking for an original copy of the game, which will generate a perfect game image instead of a violated one. The "corruption" of pirate software is not a moral issue, but a very practical one: now and then pirates have to hack (to "crack") the copy protection of the original title in order to make copies of it; they often change the introduction to make their names appear in the credits lists. Even when the game has not been hacked, technical problems can occur in the act of dumping – many of the game images floating around the Net are badly or over – dumped (so that the checksum is wrong). The more a game system was popular, the more hacked, cracked and damaged are its games – so it is hard to imagine how messy the preservation landscape for systems like Commodore 64, Nintendo Entertainment System or Nintendo Game Boy may be.

Luckily, dumpers in the age of retrogaming are aware of the negative implications of bad dumping, since the name of a dumper who preserves fixity is much more respected that the one of a dumper who does not. There are many sites on the Net whose purpose is to correctly re-dump old titles, which are available on the Net, but only in a wrong/corrupted format/version.

2.5. The perils of power

As far as cartridges are concerned, it is clear that the simple act of dumping them into ROM images creates a new menace to their fixity: they are converted from a read-only format into a read/write one. An image is nothing but a file, and as long as the file is stored on a read/write storage medium, it can be easily modified.

Apart from emulators, amateur programmers share a huge number of emulation-related utilities on the Net which let you alter a ROM image in several ways. These utilities, which often support intuitive interfaces *à la* Adobe Photoshop, can be used to modify texts and graphics, and to edit new game levels, too, even without having any knowledge of real programming languages. The risks of giving such powerful tools to every potential retrogamer is that some of the homebrew "fakes" may be mistaken for original games, thus creating confusion between what has been officially released and what has not. It is difficult to avoid getting fooled by the simplest game hacks (erotic parodies of Pac-Man, Nintendo games where original enemies are replaced with Sony or Sega characters and so on), still there are some cases where it is really hard to tell where the truth lies. For example, many Japanese RPGs never released in the West get an English homebrew translation, and this translation is often so good that the game may really look and feel like an official western release. Anyway, these good translation hacks have to be praised, because, thanks to them, a huge amount of users can pass over the Japanese linguistic barrier and enjoy some great pieces of videogaming history.

2.6. Headers and reference

The latter examples show that the problem concerns something more complex than just the concept of fixity. With so many old game systems, good dumps, bad dumps, graphics hacks, homebrew translations, and high-mortality Internet game archives, the notion of game identity itself tends to become pointless. One can download more than a hundred different Pac-Man versions from the Net, and since the joy of the retrogamer lies in collecting, it would be nice to know exactly *where* the difference lies.

Anyway, even if Internet meanders may complicate our effort of preserving videogames, the digital landscape offers revolutionary tools for archiving data. Just think about the most common operating systems: the very moment a file is created, lots of reference information is automatically stored together with it: date, size, the type of application you need to run it and so on. This kind of information is surely important when we are archiving files into our hard disk, but it becomes even more important when we deal with meta-archives like the Internet. The idea is that identity info about a game image can be stored together with it, inside a special region of the file called *header*.

Headers work in a fashion similar to DNA, but while a living being has its genetic code reproduced in every cell, a game image stores its identity info in a unique area, usually the first chunk of bytes, once and for all.

There are two types of header: the native one and the added one. Native headers have been inserted in the storage medium of the game since the game format was originally planned. They were used by the system and processed during the BIOS sequence, while the player could not have access to them. Emulators generally give the user the freedom to read such data, so that, comparing data from similar titles, one can easily spot the differences. For example, the header from a Super

Nintendo Entertainment System tells us about the title of the cartridge, the type of ROM memory employed, the presence or the absence of special math coprocessor inside the cart, the memory size of the game, the kind of TV set the game was designed for (PAL, NTSC, Secam), the game developers, the version, and the cart checksum.

Unfortunately, some of videogames of the older system did not use headers: the game code was just put on the storage medium as raw data. This may create serious problems to emulators, since they cannot look into the header for some vital info, simply because there is no header. Nintendo Entertainment System emulation is still incomplete because NES ROM dumps do not store any info about the bank switching techniques used by the game developers; since there are over 200 bank switching configurations, and a great lack of documentation, the evolution of NES emulation is very slow.

Added headers are meant to make up for this lack of info. As the name suggests, these headers do not come with the original game: they are patched to the game only after it has been transferred into an image file, to ease the job of a device (ie a copier) or an application (ie an emulator) with appropriate extra data. The difficulty of this task is to create a standard, since sometimes different emulators use different headers for an image coming from the same game system, as in the case of disk images from the Famicon Disk System. Anyway, there is plenty of de-babelizing utilities, and usually emulators are able to read more than one standard: the target is to avoid every sort of "war of the standards", so that every retrogamer can get the maximum benefit. Many people on the Net are also trying to create a "universal name standard" by inserting special tags into the file name.

3. Preservation agents on the Net: emulators

3.1. Malleable preservation tools

The second part of this essay mainly focused on the preservation object: the game image. Anyway, even perfect archives of game images are quite pointless without an emulator which lets us have real access to the software. We'll now try to explain where the power of emulation lies; finally, we shall present one of the best cases of emulation, well balanced between power and control.

Emulators become malleable objects once they are inserted in the Internet context. While it is important to obtain some form of fixity into videogame images, an emulator should be in an ever-changing evolutive process, so that it can always be adapted to a new computer or operative system.

Here are some details which further explain this concept of malleability; of course, not every emulator can enjoy all the following conditions – but the best ones for preservation purposes surely can.

– *Portability*. Many emulators are written in C++, so that the source code can be easily ported via compiler to various operative systems, by appropriately modifying only the OS-dependant factors. Moreover, many authors of emulators are loyal to the open source philosophy: they make the source code freely available on the Net, so that another programmer can submit his/her changes to the original code, or submit a porting to some other OS. Gamers can co-operate too, by posting comments, ideas, and bug reports. There are sites devoted entirely to the gathering of this kind of user's feedback.

– *Passion*. No programmer gets paid for programming the freeware emulators which flood the Internet. It is just a hobby, which may lead to some disadvantages, yet also many advantages. It is true that an emulator project can be discontinued at any time if its programmer loses interest in it. Anyway, there is not any "time to market" deadline or any "final release" waiting to come out, so that the program can be improved *ad libitum*. It may take years, but a slowly developed emulator made with passion is most likely a better deal than a commercial release quickly put together to ride a retrogaming wave. Another good thing of the passionate approach is that it is most unlikely that an old system may be forgotten because its emulator gets discontinued. After all, people want to *play* those games, and other retrogaming maniacs with programming skills will be surely glad to inherit the task of completing the emulation process.

– *Recursive emulation*. While emulated systems are somewhat 'dead' (it is not completely true, but let's make a temporary approximation), there are always new potential emulating systems, with newer and newer Operating systems and programming platforms which ask for attention. Let's now suppose that portability and passion mechanisms fail their mission, and that new OSses become destitute of some emulator gaming systems of the past: there would still be a great chance for preservation, that is, to emulate a computer system for which those emulators are available. For example, by emulating a Pentium class processor, we could access to every emulator which was conceived to run on that processor. This means that, with a single emulator, we can potentially run thousands of games and applications, which will likewise run under emulation. A new problem crops up here: who will preserve all present emulators from the dust of time? Who is "watching" after the watchers themselves? The side effect of a double-framed emulation is that we have to deal with double-framed preservation issues.

– *Free documentation*. A programmer who wants to create his/her homebrew emulator has the task of obtaining lots of hard-to-find information, especially if he/she is the first person who tries to emulate a particular system. This research is good for the whole emulation scene, since the resulting documentation is finally shared by retrogamers – after all, the source of much of this information is often the scene itself, which obviously wants to be paid back for this service. Apart from the source code for many emulators (which is anyway a great piece of documentation about the emulated system), retrogaming sites offer lots of text files which explain how to hack a cartridge copy protection, how the memory addresses a certain CPU work and so on. So, even if portability, passion and recursive emulation fail, a new emulation project would not have to start from scratch anymore. It is most likely that this documentation cannot be claimed for a copyright infringement, since it comes from a reversed engineering process, just like the emulator itself.

3.2. The road to preservation

We talked about many of the virtues of preserving videogames via emulation. But this virtuous balance did not come out of the blue. It was the result of some people'sefforts , who greatly influenced the emulation scene to promote a real preservation sub-culture, rather than a gaming-oriented one.

Marat Fayzullin, author of several emulators of Z-80 based consoles and computer systems, is remembered for his promotion of the concept of open source into emulation scene about 1995. His emulators were released under the so called "General Public Licence", a document written by the MIT researcher Richard Stallman to promote freedom in software:

> When we speak of free software, we are referring to freedom, not price. Our General Public Licenses are designed to make sure that you have the freedom to distribute copies of free software (and charge for this service if you wish), that you receive source code or can get it if you want it, that you can change the software or use pieces of it in new free programs; and that you know you can do these things. (Stallmann 1991)

Moreover, Fayzullin chose to use only freeware development tools, like the Allegro software library and the DJGPP compiler. Both applications were quite new and not very well known by the mid-Nineties: by promoting their use, the skilful programmer offered to many people the chance of making their own emulator without buying more expensive tools.

The introduction of this mechanism was very important because the making of emulators was somehow obscure; therefore, it was absolutely necessary to create a network of shared code and documentation, as well as to promote some cheap – but good developing tools. Thanks to these factors, lots of programmers got into emulation. With more emulators for more game systems of the past, more gamers joined the scene too, trying to co-operate to make everything better and bigger. By introducing a programming philosophy, Fayzullin encouraged the settling of a virtual community.

3.3. M.A.M.E.

Anyway, even if a preservation mechanism was starting to work, retrogamers were not aware of it yet – they were still mainly focused on the need of gaming. Moreover, Fayzullin's aims were not ambitious enough to push the open-source virtuous circle to its maximum. After all, he only wanted to build some computer and console emulators based on the same CPU core, so that he could manage it all alone, with relative stress on cooperation among programmers.

The rules of the game were changed at the beginning of 1997 by an Italian talented programmer named Nicola Salmoria. His target was to emulate a certain number of coin-ops from the late Seventies/early Eighties, which all used the Z-80 CPU. He started by examining the source from several single-game emulators, made by a programming group he belonged to, the Arcade Emulation Repository Project.

He decided to equip his emulator with a driver-oriented structure. Even if coin-ops he was interested in were running on similar hardware, there were still big differences between them. Each emulated game would have accessed to the same CPU emulation core, but then there would have been different drivers to emulate the specifics of every single arcade machine separately; so it was possible to let a single emulator run several games. On 2 February 1997, the Multi Arcade Machine Emulator (M.A.M.E.) was born. It was freeware, open source, written in C++ and thus easily portable. Moreover, it dealt with arcade machines, and this was quite a new and exciting thing in the emulation scene, since, for retrogamers, the wildest childhood dream was to have a real coin-operated videogame in their bedroom. M.A.M.E., at its first release on the Net, was offering 5 games, thus exceeding childhood expectations. In three years, those 5 games would have become *two thousands*, always run by a single executable file.

Emulation of the first titles was still really preliminary; Nicola thought that the driver structure would have encouraged other programmers to submit suggestions and contributions, since it was not necessary to deal with the whole program code, but only with the driver of interest, so that submitting points could be easily advanced. Nicola was even more right than he was thinking: not only did several programmers contribute to make existing drivers work better, but they also joined the M.A.M.E. project and started writing drivers on their own, feeling at ease thanks to the intelligent architecture of the emulator. Soon a new CPUs emulation was achieved, so that emulated games were no longer limited to the Z-80 family. At the same time, a porting policy of M.A.M.E. began, so that also Mac, Linux, BeOS users (with more to come) could enjoy the return of coin-op classics.

Users had a fundamental role, too. The group of people who was going to become the M.A.M.E. Team encouraged players to spot the differences between the original coin-ops and their emulated counterparts. A minor sound or graphics glitch, a strange movement pattern of an enemy are very difficult things to notice in a videogame, unless you are a maniac of that game. Fortunately, the Retrogaming scene was composed of plenty of game maniacs, that is, plenty of potential serious, expert beta-testers able to catch emulation bugs on the fly. Soon it became a common practice for M.A.M.E. programmers to emulate games they had never heard of, simply because ROM images were available and fans wanted to see that particular game emulated.

By the beginning of year the 2000, M.A.M.E. supported the emulation of 33 different CPUs, while more than 200 programmers submitted at least one contribution. Beta testers are countless. The ever-growing amount of people involved in the project sped up the emulation process a lot (a new public beta is released almost every two weeks); but M.A.M.E. evolution should not be measured by the number of games it emulates or by its big numbers in general. All these people working together had the chance to experiment on lots of programming strategies, trying to implement new options to make M.A.M.E. more than an emulator. Maybe because of a growing awareness of preservation issues, or because the emulated games were so many that it became difficult to manage them, M.A.M.E. had to turn into a strong preservation instrument, a sort of interactive document capable of processing old games from several points of view, letting the user have access to otherwise denied information. For example, M.A.M.E. can generate screenshots of every moment of the game, as well as text files with detailed technical and historical information. There are several built-in cheat options, which allow one to change every game parameter by using temporary ROM patches.

Are we reading into M.A.M.E. Team actions a preservation effort which is not really there? This is certainly not the case. Between gaming and preservation priorities, Salmoria and his colleagues always chose the latter. The typical example of this attitude concerns speed: M.A.M.E. is slow but accurate, while other emulators use some speed hacks to obtain a smoother emulation, nonetheless sacrificing some of the original inner mechanisms of the emulated machine. After all, here is an interesting statement by Salmoria, which should cast new light on M.A.M.E.'s real purposes:

> I was really interested by the technical difficulties involved. Soon after I started, I realized that information on the hardware was severely lacking and impossible to find in most cases, ROM sets were often damaged or incomplete, and so on. Therefore I decided to start the *large scale collection of information* which is now known as MAME. (Kevhal 1998)

The same spirit can be found in the opening text of the document which comes with every copy of the emulator:

> MAME is strictly a no profit project. Its main purpose is to be a reference to the inner workings of the emulated arcade machines. This is done for *educational purposes* and to *preserve many historical games* from the oblivion they would sink into when the hardware they run on will stop working. Of course to preserve the games you must also be able to actually play them; you can see that as a *nice side effect*. (M.A.M.E. Team 1998)

3.4. Beyond M.A.M.E.

Through the years, M.A.M.E. has been capable of spreading its credo in a vast part of the emulation scene. Obviously, not every open-source emulation project is as successful as Salmoria's, simply because there are some priorities inside preservation which must be respected. For instance, a very popular activity among retrogamers is to create Nintendo Entertainment System emulators, even if there are already two dozen of them around the Net; it is obvious that the task of preserving a yet unemulated coin-op is very appealing to many people.

Someone else is trying to create even more ambitious projects than M.A.M.E., which capture very well the inspirer's philosophy (and even something else) . The name for this project is M.E.S.S, an acronym for "Multi Emulator Super System". M.E.S.S. heavily exploits the source code from M.A.M.E: CPUs' emulation, driver structure, sound drivers, and everything else; anyway, its target is not set in the coin-op world, but in that of the home videogame entertainment and computing. This emulator, once again created by a team (which features also several people from M.A.M.E), aims to emulate as many console and computer systems as possible, above all those systems which really risk being forgotten, such as the Bally Astrocade, Mattel Aquarius and other memorabilia.

The project is extremely interesting, even if it is very difficult to plan the peripheral and keyboard emulation of more than a hundred systems – while M.A.M.E. coin-ops mostly share a similar interface layout (a joystick and a bunch of buttons), every console (and even worse) computer has a somewhat different way of interacting with the user. M.E.S.S. could really be the next big thing into the emulation world, since its purpose is to become "the only emulator you need". Excluding M.A.M.E., of course.

4. The best of the possible preservations?

This work has tried to explain what retrogaming is, and why it is so important for the preservation of videogames. Started as a fashion, a nostalgic revival for grown-ups, it soon turned out to be a very significant tool in digital preservation. Above all, the present work has attempted to stress the importance of the emulation projects, which are the children of the Internet virtual community called "emulation scene". From software to hardware, retrogamers on the Net continuously search for the best preservation techniques. The Community is highly aware of these issues, thanks to the efforts made by such projects as M.A.M.E., which set new preservation standards and spread concepts like "information and data sharing" and "open source".

We think that one of the most controversial points of our work is that the Internet is seen here as a tool to preserve digital objects. While everyone seems to agree that computers are crucial in preserving data, it is difficult to imagine the chaos of the Net as something useful to create reliable archives – in this case of videogames. The pace of obsolescence on the Web is really fast, not only as regards archives. Programming languages and protocols evolve as quickly as hardware. Is the Internet a good stage on which to play the "future of memory", or is it only a Babelian library dystopia?

In our opinion, this way of seeing things may be misleading. Actually, the Internet is a new medium, and the process of understanding its features and potentialities is only at the beginning. It took time for people to see the real pros of the *volumen* over the *codex,* and we think that we are facing a revolution that has a similar social and cultural meaning. Many people still fail to see that digital media are not here to substitute books and paper – they are different media with different aims.

What the Internet can do to preserve videogames is not what traditional, hierarchical archives could do. The Net offers us a whole different set of tools, and it's up to us to find the best way of using them and think of new chances of preservation to be implemented on this new medium. Our idea is that retrogamers are doing a good job, because they really know the context where games preservation is going on. They know that games are "multimedia monsters", which need lots of care and attention to keep all their content alive. Since the digital landscape is going to offer more and more multimedia objects, it would be very good for people interested in digital preservation to keep an eye on the way retrogamers are working. Their game is a very serious practice, as well as a great example of how to use the features of a new medium in preserving a very complex kind of digital text.

Internet Documents quoted

Boris, D.
1999 *Emulating Pong*, from <www.emuviews.com> (downloadable until 20/9/99).

Kevhal, V.
1998 *Interview with con Nicola Salmoria*,
<www.user.globalnet.co.uk/~kevhal/maview.html>
(downloadable until April 13, 1998)

M.A.M.E. Team
1998 *Usage and Distribution License (Readme.txt)*, stored inside this archive:
<http://www.mame.net/oldmame.html>

Stallmann, R.
1991 *GNU General Public License Version 2*, Free Software Foundation, Cambridge (US), <www.fsf.org/copyleft/gpl.html>

Task Force on Archiving Digital Information
1996 *Preserving Digital Information*,
<http://www.rlg.org/ArchTF/tfadi.index.htm>

General online resources

Because of the high mortality of Internet sites, it is quite important to quote further resources which may be useful to explore retrogaming topics.

Web sites

Daily News on emulation, news archives, emulators: *Zophar's Domain* <www.zophar.net>, *Retrogames* <www.Retrogames.com>, *Vintagegaming* <www.vintagegaming.com>, *Monroe's world* <www.monroeworld.com>, Emu Unlimited <www.emuunlim.com>. These web pages also offer many links to other interesting pages, so they are a good way to start a search.

Release dates, information about game developers and producers, reviews of old games: *All Games guide* <www.allgame.com>, *the Killer List of Videogames* <http://www.klov.com>.

Technical information about coin-ops: the best source is always the latest release of M.A.M.E. <www.mame.net>; anyway, quite useful sites are also *The Arcade Cabinet Preservation Society* <www.emuchrist.com/ACPS/index.html>, *The CPS2 Shock Technical Info* <http://geoshock.dhs.org/~haze>.

General information on *console* ed *home computer*: M.E.S.S. <mess.emuverse.com>. This project is for home systems what M.A.M.E is for coin-ops.

Anonymous Login FTP archives filled with images and other documents

ftp://Arnold.hiof.no (Commodore 64)
ftp://ftp.apple.asimov.net (Apple II)
ftp://ftp.funet.fi (for various computers and consoles)
ftp://ftp.nvg.unit.no (ZX Spectrum and Amstrad CPC)
ftp://matrix.ibb.wav.pl/pub/a8 (8 bit Atari machines)

Newsgroups

alt.binaries.emulators (amiga, cbm, gameboy, misc, neogeo, nintendo, nintendo-64, sega, tg16), it.binari.emulatori, comp.binaries.cbm: image posts

alt.emulators (amiga, classic-arcade, freemware, uae), comp.emulators (announce, apple2, cbm, freemware, game-consoles, mac.executor, misc, ms-windows.wine), it.comp.software.emulatori, tin.it.computer.emulatori: all-purpose retro-newsgroups

Seamus Ross

DIGITAL PRESERVATION: STRATEGY,
INTERVENTION, AND ACCIDENT

1. Introduction

The preservation and reuse of digital data and information forms both the cornerstone of future economic growth and development, and the foundation for the future of memory. We are increasingly aware of the economic value of information and the variety of ways it can be repackaged, marketed, and reused. This paper is concerned not with the effect of digital[1] data and information on economic growth but with the influence it will have on the memories of who we were. Investigations and views of the past depend upon access to information and wherever possible access to contemporary information. In the past these records, created as letters, chronicles, legal documents, diaries and charters, were inscribed in clay, chiselled into stone, and written on papyrus, animal skin (e.g. parchment) and paper. Computers and network-based communication, and the technologies that they enable, such as databases, geographical information systems, electronic mail and web-based interactions, are transforming the records we create, how we create them, and how we keep them.

This increasing dependence upon digital information is having several dramatic effects. First, it is changing the way in which our culture is recorded; there is no longer necessarily a direct relationship between the physical and logical structure of data and its interpretation. Second, our culture itself is being transformed; the internet has created an environment in which new communities and social groups can evolve as well as protocols and etiquette governing virtual social interaction.[2] Simply, digital information is a cultural product, d-facts or e-facts, and it forms an essential fragment of our cultural record (Ross 1993: 1). D-facts are fragile. They must be interpreted (using software and hardware) before they can be manipulated or rendered for display (or printing) and as a result in their raw form they are of little value and often meaningless. Information stored in digital form is as delicate as archaeological remains of flora and fauna – it is rare to discover them, the environmental conditions under which they were deposited influences their survival, their recovery and study depends upon substantial investment of labour, and their interpretation requires a vast array of scientific techniques. Preservation of digital information requires active intervention; left unsecured it is susceptible to loss through the physical breakdown of the media, rendered inaccessible by technological advances, or left meaningless through lack of or insufficient contextual evidence.[3]

'Where there is an economic advantage in reusing information there will be an easy business case for' its preservation.[4] The near term value of digital information or records often reflects particular regulatory environments or specific types of industry or organisation. In the financial sector records are retained on average for seven years, but in the nuclear and pharmaceutical industries records are required for business purposes over far longer periods. Data created as part of drug development (e.g. clinical trial data) needs to be retained for decades to comply with requirements established by regulatory authorities (Lord 1997: 168-174). Nuclear dump and reactor data will be valuable for hundreds if not thousands of years, where, for instance, it provides evidence for contaminated land.[5] In the automotive and aircraft industries engineering and manufacturing data need to be retained for the life of the product (and not just during the period during which the product is being made) to protect companies in the event of product liability lawsuits.[6] Satellite images are a good example of unique time-sensitive data that can not be recreated when lost. Where images taken by NASA in the 1970s of the Amazon Basin are still accessible they contribute evidence to the understanding of change over time in rain-forest coverage and density.[7] Even where records can be recreated from their analogue originals it is expensive to do so. At the 1995 meeting of the ISO Archiving Standards working group it was reported that it cost (including labour) about $5-7 per megabyte per year to retain electronic records created in the engineering sector, but about $1250 to reconstruct them if they were lost or destroyed.[8] Petroleum survey records are even more expensive to recreate. The National Archives of Australia hold 600,000 computer tapes containing oil survey data. These data are regularly reused by oil exploration companies; recreating the off-shore data would have cost in the early 1990s AUS$10,000 per metre or AUS$10 billion in total (Stuckey: 97-100). Of course the possibility of recreating information from analogue sources applies to a decreasing percentage of digital data as much tends, like satellite imagery, to be borne digital and never to have existed in analogue form.

It must be obvious that the electronic aspects of our culture targeted for preservation are those materials that have evidential value in the event of litigation, have commercial reuse value (e.g. digital film[9] or petroleum survey data), or are valued for their contribution to corporate or national memory (e.g. in the United States presidential emails). Little of the web-based literature,[10] net-based advertising, online databases, newsgroups, chat-rooms, virtual communities, music recordings, websites (including webcams), and digital images, which characterise the creations of the several hundred million internet users, are being preserved. This is hardly surprising in such a fluid environment.

Electronic mail (email), for instance, has transformed communication practices.[11] Communication is faster. We can communicate with a broader community and with individuals drawn from across much of the globe. The kinds of materials we can use to construct messages now ranges from audio to moving images to text and to virtual reality. Just as surviving correspondence enriches the writing of social historians so their digital equivalent, email, will provide a valuable source for future historians.[12] In reconstructing the past historians have always used a great diversity of sources. For example, Jean-Jacques Aubert (1994) investigated papyri from public and private archives, epigraphic inscriptions, archaeological remains, and literature to produce his elegant study of Roman Business Managers. The dry facts stripped from archival documents were given life through the judicious use of satirical quotations from Roman playwrights (e.g. Plautus). In common with other historians he pulled together the residue of past; evidence distilled and teased from fragmentary documentary sources, artefacts, and art historical materials. We recognise that to know who we are and the impact of our past on our future we need to know where we came from. As a consequence the approaches to constructing stories about the past and the kinds of stories historians build are varied.[13] In our multi-cultural society this richness of approach reflects the resources we are creating and the expectations of the world in which we live. Historians of the future will seek out chat-room transcripts, newsgroups, emails, webcams, and websites along-side company and government records, credit and health data sets, and registers.

In general, historic records survive more often by accident than by design. The burning of the Persian palace-site of Persepolis after its fall to Alexander, for example, although a savage act of vandalism, contributed to the preservation of the palace archives. In the 1930s excavators recovered this archives inscribed on unfired clay tablets. Under most conditions clay tablets are, by their nature, more durable than other types of media. The Persepolis tablets were written to track economic transactions; the scribes who recorded them would perhaps have been surprised that by analysing these thousands of tablets it proved feasible to profile the position and role of women in ancient Persia under Darius I to Artaxerxes III.[14] Sadly only a percentage of these tablets have been fired since their discovery in the 1930s and many are reported to be drying out and crumbling away in their new home at the Oriental Institute at the University of Chicago. The content of many of the tablets has not yet been transcribed; mere recovery of media does not necessary protect it or its contents against loss. Indeed, recovery may, in fact, expose the material to new dangers. Likewise, we move our digitally encoded information from one decaying medium to another equally unsuitable media type or from one archaic encoding format to another soon to be superseded format.[15] The medium and form of clay tablets, and their content and its structure, raise comparative issues of media durability, content visibility and intelligibility, metadata,[16] 'contextual metadata drift', data recovery, and technological obsolescence.

The structure, form and incisions on clay tablets indicate the presence of information, even if we prove unable to decipher it. Digital storage media, on the other hand, give little clue to the presence or format of the data they contain, and only occasionally an indication of what devices might be needed to access them.[17] Preserving digital assets cannot happen as an after-thought, it must be planned: media degrade (e.g. magnetic particles lose their properties and dye layers on optical media break down),[18] technological developments make systems obsolete,[19] or information is rendered inaccessible by changes in encoding formats (Ross & Gow 1999: 11-13).[20] The near-term economic and productivity advantages offered by digital storage, manipulation, and communication encourages us to depend on them more and more. Although we are aware of the preservation risks, society in general ignores them.

2. The landscape

We have reached a turning point in the production, distribution, and handling of recorded information. We now create resources in digital form:

- that can be easily distributed and refreshed;
- that do not suffer loss of fidelity when copied or used;
- the integrity of which can be secured and verified;
- that can be analysed using an array of automated processing tools; and,
- which can be searched with increasing degrees of sophistication and accuracy.

Contemporary society creates two classes of digital material: the results of retrospective conversions, and resources created only in digital form.

The belief that scholarship and society benefit from the availability of high quality digital resources and networked access to them is reflected in the increasing emphasis that academic institutions, public archives and libraries, commercial media companies, and funding agencies put on the retroconversion of material.[21] Watching these activities one senses the wholesale rush to retroconvert our documentary heritage into virtual form without a realisation that we are potentially exposing this material to an increased risk of loss. On the other hand with eighty percent, including some ten million unique scholarly publications in American research libraries printed on acidic paper the quantity of material in need of rescue is immense.[22] Although branded with its own inherent risks digitisation offers the best way to address the preservation and access problems posed by material on acidic paper. In addition projects are digitising millions of archival documents, architectural drawings, newspapers, photographs, film and audio recordings and many other materials. Where digitisation is inappropriate projects are keying the data. Retroconversion is an expensive process. The resource implications and the technical challenges mean that contemporary librarians and archivists face major problems in deciding what of our cultural heritage should be retrospectively converted (Ross 1999b: 5-27).[23] Hundreds of retroconversion projects of all different sizes and types are now underway. Hundreds of millions of euros are being invested in these projects.

The diversity of approaches, the variety of technologies and management practices, and range of funding models are reflected in these ten example projects: The British Library's Beowulf Project,[24] The Archivo General de Indias (González 1999), the Music Performance Research Centre,[25] and the Cornell Digitisation programme,[26] Beazley Archive,[27] the Scottish Archives Network (SCAN),[28] JSTOR,[29] American Memory Project,[30] Duderstadt Archive (Ebeling & Thaller ,eds., 1999),[31] and Bibliothèque Nationale de France (Cathaly 1998: 15- 19).[32] These and many other projects are increasing the diversity of resources accessible to researchers and the general public. The influence that these projects will have on education, life-long learning, and scholarship will only become clear with hindsight much as happened with the substantial editing enterprises of the nineteenth century (e.g. Rolls Series, *Monumenta Germania Historica*).[33]

Approaches to publication are changing. A shift towards large scale databases, in which the results of the efforts of individual research teams can be aggregated for comparative and often interdependent analysis, has begun to take place in the sciences. The Human Genome project, which is generating a digital record of our genetic makeup, is the flagship of this kind of approach.[34] Another example, the Protein Information Resource (PIR) has since 1984 provided researchers in evolution and computational biology with access to a regularly updated, quality controlled, and detailed protein sequence database.[35] In the humanities projects, such as the Corpus of Romanesque Sculpture in Britain and Ireland (CRSBI),[36] and English Heritage's Images of England,[37] are producing digital image and data banks to improve our understanding of heritage assets and to enable new ways of investigating them. The issues of sustainability, maintenance, and enhancement are critical to the viability of these resources. These databases will be maintained so long as they have immediate public or research value, but they may not continue to be when immediate interest in them has diminished. Yet we know that information assets go through phases of value and they often regain their value in the future. Unlike many analogue resources that can survive periods of neglect these may not.

Internet Archaeology, an early and continuing experiment in electronic journal publication, reflects a radical rethink of how the results of scholarly endeavour could be presented.[38] While the electronic environment changes how research can be constructed and presented, it exposes this material to risk. Libraries do not keep copies of *Internet Archaeology*: long term access depends upon continuity of the original project. The only copy (save a few backups stored on magnetic tape in the Special Collections of the University of York Library) is the one held by the Project itself. Even though *Internet Archaeology* has rigorous data management policies, this lack of redundancy and geographic spread of copies increases the risk of loss. This problem is exacerbated by the fact that the ability to read many articles depends on specialised software (e.g. use of Cosmo player for the Virtual Reality Modelling Language (VRML)) which the project may not be able to archive. A lack of strategic planning on the part of electronic journal publishers means that results of research presented in electronic form are at risk of becoming inaccessible. Moreover as the sources on which we build our research are increasingly digitally-based, the sources themselves will not survive, will be moved to new locations, or will be moved from open access to restricted areas or on to chargeable sites. These changes increase the difficulties associated with verifying conclusions or repeating analyses: the very functionality which digital presentation should enable. One wonders whether the surviving record of scholarship will be like constructing the contents of ancient and medieval libraries from the few surviving manuscripts; we can identify the names of the titles of many works but not even a unique copy of many of these titles survives anywhere?

Far more alarming than all this has been the change in the way society now creates its documentary heritage. As Rick Barry has noted, changes in working practices are having a substantial impact on the process of document creation, their format, how they are used, and how they are managed.[39] Business activities depend on databases, digital images, geographical information systems, voice mail, email, video recordings, spreadsheets, and word-processed documents. As a result records (from an archival vantage) and information come in a plethora of types, formats, and structures. The working practices of archivists, librarians and records managers respond to a world composed of textual documents, when the business activities of their organisations now use a range of composite documents of varying complexity:

– static documents composed of such elements as text, tables, and images;

- multimedia or data-rich documents such as the kinds of documents that we encounter in the networked environment (on the world-wide web or on www-based corporate intranets); and,
- dynamic documents dependent upon data that might have variable instantiations and be held in databases and spreadsheets (Ross 1998: 7-17).

These materials form the major resources for the future of memory.

With some 800 million web pages currently (2000) accessible, including thousands linked to databases, the amount of information accessible to contemporary users of the web can only be described as astonishing.[40] Financial institutions, commercial users, and governments move even larger amounts of data across private networks and much of this is shipped from computer to computer without any human intervention. Airlines, banks, and credit-card companies handle billions of transactions each year. The data contained in the detailed record of each individual transaction provides information that could be used to profile many aspects of modern society which more traditional textual documents do not illuminate. The sheer quantity of the data, however, makes, even in a world of falling storage costs,[41] its retention difficult. Where they are retained these data could be mined in different ways.[42] Resources might be examined with change over time in mind and credit transaction data or travel information linked with, say, medical records. Researchers will use the surviving information not to understand the individual transactions recorded in the data, but the society(ies) that created them. The proven potential of data mining methods indicates that even where data have been summarised for contemporary purposes the unaggregated data should be retained because future analysis work might wish to use the primary data for new purposes. Our scribes in Persopolis retained the records of the individual transactions after they produced the summary records; it was the individual transactions which yielded their riches to scholars by allowing them to use economic data to develop cultural understandings.

From the early in1990s onwards I have drawn attention to the parochialism that pervades studies of electronic information (Ross 1997: 330-336). Archivists and records managers have focused on the preservation of records and librarians on ensuring long-term access to published resources and on-line databases. Yet, until we have a much broader acceptance of the realisation that it is essential that we preserve a broader cross-section of our digital heritage media manufacturers, system developers, and software designers will not be encouraged to introduce preservation capabilities or functionality into their products. The discussions of the issues of digital preservation must be taken beyond the traditional communities of archivists and librarians if progress is to be made in addressing the dangers.[43]

Major new initiatives are collecting data to improve the contemporary understanding of the impact of human activity on the environment and man's changing relationship with it. These resources will provide a foundation for studies of change over time. In monitoring natural phenomena (e.g. seismic or meteorological activity) or experiments scientific instruments can capture gigabytes of data every hour.[44] As a result it is not uncommon for data sets to be as large as a terabyte and it would not be impossible to collect a petabyte of data. In turn the precision of many simulations depends on hundreds of gigabytes of data. In these data sets resides information about bio-diversity, environmental conditions, and our genetic makeup. Large numerical data sets and text files represent a fraction of the uses and products of the digital environment. Designers of buildings, airplanes, and a host of products have increasingly turned to computer environments to enhance the design and testing processes. Architects and mechanical and electrical engineers depend upon computer aided design/drafting applications and virtual reality systems. A consequence of this is that architectural historians will wish to have access to this material. Unlike numerical data which can be migrated from one software/hardware environment to another access to this material will be dependent upon access to specific software tools and its interpretation will depend upon the use of original hardware or the emulation of that equipment. This is especially true of Virtual Reality models. Looking back historians will wish to see the materials in their original context, whether this must be the actual environment or whether a virtual one would prove suitable remains an open question and will depend on the nature of digital experiences in the future.

The use of computer technologies for entertainment and in particular interactive computer games is recognised as a major driving force in the race to create faster computers with better graphics.[45] Only a very small number of institutions are collecting these games and their consoles, yet they are critical cultural artefacts as they are shaping leisure behaviour and have provided the training ground for a whole generation of computer users. The violence inherent in many of these games may be playing a role in shaping our own attitudes towards violence; the preservation of the games will contribute to future researchers understanding of our culture.

On current evidence historians of the future will be left with a large number of disconnected d-facts that will prove difficult to use. In the first seminar[46] to look at these issues we investigated such questions as how much data should be retained: all possible records or just a sample of them. Martin Campbell-Kelly asked, for instance: Would a single airline reservation transaction have value to a future historian? Would it be practical to retain all the tens of millions of airline reservations for posterity? Would future historians be overwhelmed if we were to preserve all these data? Similar questions could be asked about other classes of records. A spurious analogy is frequently drawn with the way archives are currently used; faced with the vast quantities of surviving paper documents in few researchers can be comprehensive. Archives of the future will be different and researchers will adopt new, and more technology dependent, ways of working. With an array of analysis tools they will work more exhaustively with the surviving digital resources than they have so far been able to work with analogue ones. Insurance, retailing, and banking sectors currently exploit the potential of data mining techniques and tools to extract information from large heterogeneous data sets (Pyle 1999; Han 1998: 97-107). Increasingly interpreting work to interpret these data is assisted by data visualisation tools. In addition to data mining and visualisation tools future researchers will be aided by intelligent agents that explore the Internet (or its successor) looking for information that meets certain user-specified criteria and refining their searches as they accumulate data and knowledge (Maes 1999: 44-54). Digital archives combined with new technologies will liberalise scholarship; they will enable simultaneous access to a range of sources (both local and distant) and facilitate the use of research methods not possible with conventionally-printed or hand-written records.

3. Digital preservation: A proactive approach

This vision of a rich information record just waiting to be harvested and processed by the technology-enabled researcher of the future depends upon the survival of digital data. Sadly, based on current experience it is evident that not much of this digital material will survive. It is already impossible to find old documentation for early computers, such as those from the 1960s and 1970s, even if you can locate an aging machine.[47] Access to material created using superseded operating systems (e.g. CP/M) or word-processing (e.g. Wordstar) and database (e.g. Dbase III) applications is difficult. Legacy systems written in such languages as Cobol, PL/1, and Fortran are equally prone to loss and were frequently tied to particular operating systems and system calls to particular hardware devices. In the past librarians and archivists have worked to ensure that the resources we need are available for very long periods by collecting, documenting, securing, and managing them. If digital materials are to remain accessible over decades, let alone centuries, preservation features need to be incorporated into them. Records Managers have continued to raise awareness within companies about the dangers posed to corporate memory by the increased use of digital technologies. The viability of long term retention of digital materials depends, they argue, upon records management involvement in the design of new systems. Current practices do not recognise the value of the participation of preservationists in the system design phase; so the effort of records managers focuses on rescue after creation and then generally after acquisition. Even by the time digital materials are passed into the care of records managers the systems and computer hardware on which they were created are often obsolete.[48] The records could arrive on tapes (nine-track tape of varying bit-densities), cartridges (e.g.,TK50, DLTs, DAT), hard disks, floppies, solid state storage devices, or CDs. In each case a range of generations of media might be included in the deposit (e.g. 8", 5.25", and 3.52 floppies), magnetic tapes and cartridges. Of all these media the CD-ROM or CD-R is probably the easiest to handle because at least the standards have been broadly in place for nearly two decades and the drives are ubiquitous (but the low stability of the media may prove a obstacle). In other cases the media may prove inaccessible because the peripheral devices are no longer available; how many organisations have access to 8" floppy drives or quarter-inch cartridge (QIC) tape drives and appropriate software, and especially drivers to operate them. Even if it is possible to get the data from the media it will be in a range of file formats including word processing, sound, text, image, and database file formats. Little will be generic enough to be accessed without the original applications. Some of these will be proprietary and others will require particular versions of software that was long-since superseded.

Who is selecting and how they are selecting material for preservation is undergoing change. The administrative, legal, and information value of records as well as their long-term research potential are recognised as key selection criteria. In the new technology environment appraisal decisions might come to reflect technical issues including the quality of data set/resource documentation and (or) metadata, and the uniqueness of the operating system, software or hardware environment needed to access/use the data (Ross 1998).[49] Researchers can only hope that documentation is preserved so that environments can be reconstructed and the integral relationships within the discrete data units necessary to render the information resource processable can be re-established. [50] The problem is not so much that it is impossible to retain all information created in electronic form but that it is not feasible to document it suitably to ensure its long term accessibility. Unlike the Bisutun Inscription or the Rosetta Stone, where a single inscription helped unlock the records of an entire culture, much more will be required if digital materials are to be accessed in the future.

We now widely recognise that preservation is an active process and the debates about digital preservation strategies have generated a substantial quantity of literature.[51] There are numerous preservation models emerging and even systems under development, some in the libraries arena[52] and still more in the area of archives and records management.[53] The main objective of all this effort is to ensure long-term access to digital resources created by contemporary commercial companies (e.g. publishers) and public sector bodies. We expect to be able to identify, retrieve, render, and use these resources in the future and that when we seek to do so they will be complete, authentic, and verifiable (Dollar 1999). Preservation strategies that have been investigated include preservation of obsolete technologies,[54] migration of digital records to new environments,[55] emulation of obsolete systems (e.g. applications, software, and hardware),[56] bundling,[57] persistent object preservation,[58] and binary retargetable code.[59] Almost without exception preservation strategies depend upon refreshing media through replication or copying of information to new media types.[60] None of the currently available preservation solutions could be described as 'tried and tested', but work in developing modelling tools, models, and standards have begun to provide a more secure foundation for ensuring the longevity of digital objects.[61]

It is widely agreed that, if digital materials are to be preserved, then wherever possible their preservation must be an integral element of the initial design of systems (Ross 1998: 9-25). This rarely happens and most digital preservation work, as explained above, must be carried out after the resource has been created and frequently when it is no longer an operational system. Indeed part of the problem facing archives and libraries wishing to accession electronic publications is the heterogeneous nature of the materials and the lack of consistency in data, application design, documentation, and metadata. Recent efforts have concentrated on establishing digital preservation infrastructures that are platform independent and support ingesting of heterogeneous digital resources. As the researchers in the NEDLIB project have concluded solutions must be founded on a layered architecture 'that provides a clear separation between the hardware, such as storage and communication devices, the protocols and the applications', and depends upon open standards.[62] This invariably means that material will be selected for preservation and that metadata, or information that is attached to primary data to give them context and usability, will have an impact on this selection process.

In comparison to resources produced on analogue media, such as on paper, resources created in digital form are fragile and easily prone to becoming physically and logically inaccessible. The degradation of the media on which they are stored, loss of functionality of access devices, loss of manipulation capabilities, loss of presentation capabilities, or weak links in the documentation chain are all factors that contribute to making resources inaccessible (Ross & Gow 1999: iv-v). Other factors such as loss of contextual information or relevance can render resources non-interpretable. While it is true that it is feasible to recover data that have become inaccessible under many circumstances (and even to the surprise of some data creators), this can be an expensive, labour intensive and a risky approach to the resource preservation problem especially when we recognize that few data recovery methods are comprehensive or successful on every occasion. One risk is that while much data are not 'bit critical' (Swade 1993: 93-104), the same claim can not be made for most software. On the other hand just ensuring that the binary digits are intact through refreshing the media will not ensure that the digital resources can be retrieved, interpreted, manipulated and presented. Work by the Bundesarchiv (Koblenz) to recover the *Kaderdatenspeicher*, a detailed database of East German Party Officials, depended upon the survival of contextual information and in particular documentation (Wettengel 1998: 264-276). In general the digital resource is such a new concept that we have not yet had time to come to grips with its qualities in an effective and meaningful way.

What we are seeking is a strategy for ensuring the perpetual access to digital resources that protects the integrity, functionality, and meaning of digital materials. This can only occur where acquisition and management of digital resources is controlled, contextual information is secured, and sufficient preservation metadata are attached to the resource to ensure it is capable of interpretation in the future. While these are primarily technical requirements, the effectiveness with which these can be addressed depends on the organizational and managerial environment in which they are to be conducted. In other words, preservation strategies without policies will not work.

In any preservation strategy metadata will have a pivotal role as it provides the only way to capture the context of a resource and the processes defining and surrounding its use.[63] The issues associated with generating metadata sufficient to ensure digital preservation remain unresolved despite the efforts of numerous research projects. The work done on preservation metadata, although extensive, has been primarily at the theoretical level and little of it has been adequately tested on any systems of scale.[64] Metadata is a central element of any model designed to ensure that preserved data is functional. One of the problems, however, is that the complexity of inter-relationships between resources and the various software applications used to run them may be easily overlooked when creating the metadata elements of the wrapper. The representation of metadata (e.g. Reference Information and Preservation Description Information) also raises difficulties. At its highest level there are three types of metadata: preservation, bibliographic or discovery, and administrative or management.

The creation of software and hardware independent records or 'information assets' requires that all materials that are placed in the archives are linked to information about their structure, context, and use history. These metadata must be sufficient to support the migration of records through various generations of hardware and software, to support the reconstruction of the decision-making process,[65] to provide audit trails throughout a record's life cycle, to provide records with self-selecting and self-appraising characteristics, and to capture internal documentation. Conceptually metadata that needs to be attached to digital information and especially electronic records includes:

- information about the source of the data;
- details of how, why and when it was created;
- details about its intended function or purpose;
- guidelines about how to open and read the record;
- terms of access;
- the migration history of the record and any changes made to it after it was created;
- information about how it interrelated to other software and records used by the organisation or other organisations.

Within this emerging consensus there are difficulties:

- created because metadata models have not been tested across a matrix of organisational categories and data types;
- using metadata to represent the business processes (including information flow);
- associated with layers of documentation and the need for a wider coverage of system documentation;
- incorporating metadata guidelines into software; and,
- associated with ensuring future systems will be able to interpret and use these metadata.

The current definitions of the form and properties of the metadata which are useful for the management of other data often ignores issues of process and the need to define metadata in terms that reflect the specific environment in which the data was used. Metadata need to be derived from an analysis of the organisational functional requirements and needs. Only where metadata categories are derived from an analysis of the business processes can one ensure that they reflect the functional uses made of the data. Concentration on the definition of metadata divorced from the processes that need to be undertaken using metadata will result in the creation of metadata guidelines of limited value because they will not reflect the data environment. Where the metadata include evidence of the processes future users will be in a strong position to understand the role that information/data played in the organisation. The process driven model underlies the research being conducted by the DLM-Forum Working Party on functional requirements (Macfarlane 1998: 70-73).

Records exist for a purpose and these reflect the functions and activities of the creating organisation. Appraisal and selection criteria include the evaluation of the relationship between the purpose for which the record was created and the organisation's purpose. Purpose is closely related to process. Process descriptions are essential if records are to be worth retaining. This is true not only for records preserved as a record of the creating organisation's own history, but also for records retained for their informational value because they need to be contextualised in the environment in which they were used. Appraisal and selection of electronic records will also involve an evaluation of the processes that were performed on the metadata to reconstruct the original organisational processes and behaviour.

Relying on a single preservation strategy is analogous to single crop economies in an agrarian society. For instance, migration has been suggested as a primary method of digital preservation and it has been more widely reviewed than any other approach.[66] It depends upon the periodic conversion of resources from older forms into newer formats before the older formats become obsolete.[67] The appearance and behaviour of digital resources is frequently intrinsically linked to proprietary software and even hardware. For all the discussion about migration the small scale of the test-beds has not yet provided sufficient evidence to establish with any degree of confidence that such a model could be applied across a heterogeneous and changing resource base. It is this variability in the resource base and the rapid changes in the digital models that make relying on migration strategies alone risky. Furthermore as migration is very much a handcraft it makes the process of migration-based digital preservation labour intensive and therefore expensive. These costs will increase the greater the time depth between the point at which the digital asset was created and when it is to be migrated (Hendley 1998). The size of the resource does not necessarily correspond directly with the cost of its migration or emulation; a small resource that required significant labour investment could cost as much to migrate as one hundreds or thousands of times larger, but for which less intervention was necessary.

Often overlooked are the twin issues of (1) acceptable levels of loss and (2) the complexity of designing and implementing automated testing strategies to ensure the functional relationship between the digital materials before and after migration. Before we can see migration as a viable aid to preservation more work is needed in the development of metrics for benchmarking and supporting the evaluation of the risks to the functionality of the data set or losses resulting from particular changes. The question of 'how much loss is acceptable' whether this is in functionality, integrity, authenticity, or meaning has not been adequately addressed by any commercial or research initiatives. Part of the reason is that conceptually any loss is not acceptable, but practically it is difficult to operate preservation methods that avoid any. If the primary aim of the digital preservation is to ensure that future users can identify, retrieve, render, manipulate, and use resources then it is essential that loss of content, context, integrity or functionality be negligible.[68]

Whatever the longer-term preservation methods adopted for an individual resource all resources will need to be wrapped for preservation. This will involve encapsulating or linking the resource to adequate reference (e.g. description of data types, operations, relationships) and preservation description (e.g. reference, provenance, context, and fixity) information. The precise metadata requirements of each digital object will vary; the metadata required for each digital resource could be drawn from a metadata repository.[69] For instance, it is worth recognising that if a digital resource is destine for migration a different metadata set would be required from that necessary for emulation. Where intervention-based preservation is feasible preservation of digital resources depends upon a mixture of strategies: the OAIS (Open Archival Information System) model supports this diversity of approach and is currently emerging as the standard methodology.[70]

4. Digital preservation: Accident and rescue

It should be obvious that we actually understand a tremendous amount about the problems and have many ideas about how to overcome them. Apathy and lack of realisation of the urgency is leading to inaction. This trend will continue. Unfortunately neither strategically planned nor intervention-based preservation will be the norm; the most common preservation method will be 'accident'. Where digital data does survive future users will not access it in the same way contemporary users do.[71] Valuable cultural data contained in the record structures, software (e.g. applications), and hardware will hold keys to understanding the material itself, processes of work, and the culture which created the materials. Much as, from close analysis of the formulae, the internal structure, and the vocabulary of the *Donatio Constantio* the Renaissance thinker Lorenzo Valla (1440) demonstrated it was a forgery,[72] future scholars will attempt to validate their digital resources. Scholars will ask whether severing the data from the environment in which it was created and used debases the message. Even contemporary users recognise that this is the case with multimedia, geographical information systems, databases and virtual records. Without the original software to process and render the data it will be impossible to determine what kinds of (or specific) virtual records users might have created and how they were presented to them. Furthermore just as modern historians study ancient archives to understand working practices and the functioning of government administration,[73] cultural and social historians will look beyond the content of the records to understand how the tools and the environment of work conditioned the social behaviour of the workers and work.[74]

From among the long-term access methods, emulation is the most promising.[75] It will make it possible for us to experiment with historic hardware and software and understand old ways of working. One wonders how we will comprehend the misery caused to a generation of users by flickering and immobile screens, and poorly designed keyboards if we are unable to experiment with the older equipment itself. As far as hardware is concerned experiments have demonstrated that simulation does not provide the user the same level of understanding which can be provided by access to the original environment. The experience of having seen technicians use the forty-year-old Ferranti Pegasus Computer in the Science Museum (London) to perform data processing tasks provided an impression of the process of work in the late 1950s that the Computer Conservation Society simulation of the same system does not. Other well-know emulations and simulations including the ENIAC-on-a-Chip,[76] PDP-11,[77] and the EDSAC[78] demonstrate that we will be able to create unique systems.

On the other hand emulation offers the most secure way of ensuring access to data, software, and presenting the functions of older systems. My research team at HATII, have examined the growing number of sites devoted to emulation and conducted experiments and evaluations to determine the viability of system emulation and simulation. Our small scale pilots lead us to conclude that emulation offers a viable path. Larger scale experiments are necessary to confirm this assessment. These must involve, for instance, larger data sets, a more diverse range of input devices, more programming languages, programs using a greater number of system calls, applications depending upon the presence of particular hardware, and more complex software.

Even if we do nothing I doubt everything will become lost. For example even after storage under extreme conditions it is still possible to recover data from magnetic media. A team of scientists at IBM demonstrated this when NASA presented it with computer tapes from the wreck of Challenger Space Shuttle. These tapes had spent six weeks immersed in the sea off the Florida coast (Bhushan & Phelan 1987: 3179-3183. Kalthoff, Bradshaw, Bartkus & Finkelstein 1987: 4004-6). When recovered the tapes were covered in salt deposits and the magnetic coating had disappeared in some reel segments and in others the tape substrate was eroded as a result of chemical reactions. The main damage this corrosion had caused was to the adhesive of the tapes and as a result the binder and substrata were separating. Despite these deficiencies the team was able to recover the vast majority of the data after washing and chemically treating the tapes. The project team had several advantages in their favour: knowledge that there was data on the tapes to be recovered, a collection of identical undamaged media to provide chemically controlled samples, the type of hardware necessary to read the tapes, and a knowledge of the data format of the tapes. Had they found the tapes, but had none of this information their task would have been even more difficult, if they had begun at all.

What will certainly be lost where data is preserved by accident is context and we will pass onto the future a major data recovery and reconstruction problem (Robertson 1996). Techniques of digital archaeology are evolving already. The growing data recovery and computer forensic industries are building tools and methods to find, recover, and interpret data that is inaccessible. Data recovery companies have begun to stockpile components (e.g. hard drive assemblies and hard drives themselves). There is a need for generic devices to read media independently of the read-write devices used to create it. One approach that shows promise combines Magnetic Force Microscopy[79] (MFM) and cryptographic techniques. With MFM it is possible to read the magnetic media. A raw bit stream of 0s and 1s provides few clues to how it is to be interpreted let alone its meaning; low level context information such as block size, encoding standards, and file structure, will prove essential (see Note 24). It might be feasible to draw out a text document or a data set relatively easily, but a digital image whose format was completely unknown and appearing as a single bit stream would require significant analysis before it could be rendered. Here a great deal more research into cryptographic analysis will be required. The nature of digital representation for storage makes data stored in this way particularly susceptible to cryptographic methods of analysis.

The internet and the web pose new problems to future historians. Until recently most digital information was created inside companies and government organisations, but this is beginning to change. The internet has provided us with a new environment for information creation and exchange. Preserving webpages and online databases would be challenging especially where the information that user's view is dynamically generated in response to particular queries or information provided. Government organisations have begun to address the preservation of their webpages especially where the webpages are records.[80] The internet is more than webpages and it is these other aspects that will prove the most difficult to preserve and for future researchers to reconstruct. More dramatically the internet has enabled an environment in which we can have new kinds of social experiences, where we can take part in new communities, and where the concepts, function and role of imagination, gender, ethnicity, identity and community are taking on new meanings and contexts. Preserving the computer boxes, screens, routers, wires, programmes and applications will not make it possible for future historians to comprehend this phenomena and its transformative impact. The relationship between the function of these objects and the behaviour of the user in general or within specific virtual environments is likely to remain opaque. For example, how will future scholars understand virtual and real world identities when the former are likely to be multiple, dynamic and unrecorded. This virtual world is changing so fast that behaviours that were evident and observable five years ago have disappeared because the environment has shifted the behavioural goal-posts. The internet and the culture experiences it provides both reflects real communities and permits us to experience worlds not otherwise open to us.

Other factors are putting digital memory at risk. Fear of legal action encourages organisations to destroy data in their care.[81] Even in countries where the necessity to preserve digital materials is recognised, legal constraints, such as the framing of the EU Data Protection Directive, are making it increasing difficult to retain certain kinds of data. A significant obstacle to digital access and preservation is Intellectual Property Rights (IPR). Moreover, the trend towards ownership of knowledge as though it were a tangible property poses new problems (Shulman 1999). We are fast becoming a knowledge economy in which data, information and knowledge about how these resources can be used is more important than tangible products. Ownership of knowledge restricts its dissemination and decreases the likelihood of its survival.[82] Alongside these are other risks including encryption and viruses.[83] Encryption is particularly a concern because while we may secure raw data for the future we may make it inaccessible as the decryption algorithms, software, or keys become separated from the data itself. Computer viruses and related programs, while they may pose a threat to present and future data and systems, need to be preserved because they tell us much about contemporary counter-culture.

5. Conclusion

Increasingly our culture and its by-products are represented as binary digits. These digital materials are at risk of loss or of becoming inaccessible unless they are properly monitored, managed, and secured. We know what can be done to improve the chances that digital data will survive and the areas where further research could make us even better able to preserve digital materials. It is unlikely, however, that much material will be preserved by design. Accident is more likely to provide the mode of preservation as it has in the past. Whether the material survives by accident or design the survival of documentation about our culture is likely to become increasingly important to a larger and larger segment of the population. In post-industrial countries a growing segment of the population pursue activities that involve genealogy and the study of family history and take part in other life-long learning activities. Their interests extend well-beyond merely tracing lineage. They wish to know more about how they and their ancestors fit into the culture, community, and world in which they live(d).

As a consequence, research and scholarship in the future is likely to be more personal. It will be more about configuring stories that tell us who we are and where we came from. Whether this is our social history, our ability to chart our place in demographic change, to review our medical history and that of our community overtime, to study the diet of our immediate and distant ancestors. In many ways history is an attempt to build an interpretative structure on the debris left by others. Over the past 150 years the richness and nature of that layer has changed dramatically as new disciplines have been created (from social history to demography to women's studies). All has depended upon new interpretative methods, been related to the changing attitudes of the contemporary world, and most importantly been built on larger and more diverse data, whether these data are: artefacts, ecofacts, charters, diaries or whatever. The interpretative layers have tended towards the general. New ways of working and new technologies will change all this. Currently through our two classes of digital materials – retroconversion, and new digital content much of which is the by-products of contemporary life – we have just started creating the digital record we need for the future. In the not too distant future I will be able to choose from a virtual catalogue a 'virtual researcher' who (and actually I should have written which, but I have already begun to anthropomorphise our 'virtual scholar') will be able to traverse this digital landscape and collect and analyse all this data/ information/records to construct interpretative layers within defined structures. These tireless, nimble, and adaptive knowledge builders will be able to examine massive data sets to do such things as study environmental records, chemical dumping and nuclear waste data to help us to understand better how we have destroyed our planet and to help us to plan its future use. Most importantly they will allow future generations to examine the relationship between their individual ancestors, events and a wider range of societal phemonena. Any future scholarship depends upon the survival of the digital resources, and their survival in accessible and intelligible contexts. This is currently a far greater challenge than any study of the past has ever been. How should we tackle this problem? We must engage the popular imagination in the possibilities opened through the preservation of digital assets. We must encourage media, software, and hardware developers to think long-term. We must encourage those creating data to recognise their long-term value and act to secure them for the future. We must recognise that no single community will address the problems of digital preservation in isolation. Without an answer our past will become either the property of an economic elite while the majority of us are fed a pulp of edutainment or it will be, to paraphrase Herodotus, 'blotted from memory'.

This examination of digital information and its long term accessibility allows us to reach six general conclusions:

- we already know a tremendous amount about how we can assist the longer term preservation of the digital products of our culture and we need to use this knowledge effectively and strategically to improve the chances that they will survive;

- while we can assist future researchers wishing to access data created by our culture by ensuring that our digital products are documented, rich in metadata, and created using open standards, digital information will survive more often by accident than by design;

- during the next couple of decades there will be a growth in digital archaeology and data recovery tools and methods in response to the increasing amounts of unsecured digital information;

- the internet is fast changing all assumptions about digital preservation as it is creating new environments which lead to the creation of significant cultural data outside organisations that are likely to preserve them and it fosters behaviours and interactions which often leave no sustainable traces;

- we need to consider the time-frame for which we are hoping to sustain our digitally encoded memories and decide what is really viable and what is really necessary; and,

- in the short-term, say the next fifty to one hundred years, technological and methodological developments will enable researchers to use surviving digital resources far more comprehensively than has been possible with analogue resources in the past.

Our digitally encoded memories are fast becoming obsolete and as we create more and more ingenious ways of encoding and storing them we tend to exacerbate the preservation problem. While we should act positively to address these difficulties we must not underestimate the lengths to which future generations will go to unravel the record we leave behind. We must also not forget how evocative a single record can be to the future. In 1988 I visited the archaeological site of Boxgrove in Southern England. Some 300,000 years earlier a hunter-gather had squatted below the flint-clay cliffs, which latter sealed the site, and made a flint tool. Not long after the fragments of flint, which had been chipped away in the process, were covered by sand. As a result of painstaking effort, archaeologists were able from the distribution of the flint fragments to reconstruct the tool that had occupied this ancestor for twenty or thirty minutes and to even detail which of the tool-makers hands had been predominant. We would wish future generations not to have a patchy record of our culture; we should act responsibly to ensure that we are leaving a digital record to the future which is durable, processable, and intelligible.

Notes

[1] In this paper the terms digital and electronic are used interchangeably when referring to data, information, and knowledge. The term 'records' is used primarily in an archives and records management sense.

[2] The Humanities Advanced Technology and Information Institute at the University of Glasgow 1999/2000 seminar, *Investigating Cyberspace: Communities and Cultures on the Net*, examined the growth and nature of communities in cyberspace and the evolution of social behaviour within them. While a number of authors have examined the formation of net-based cultures and have described methods for examining and describing them these methods and theories remain in a formative stage. (See for instance: Dery 1996; Jones 1997; Porter 1997; Rheingold 1995; and Turkle 1997). The more significant aspect of the problems is, however, that as the residue of this culture is digital its survival is unlikely. There is little that will be left to future historians from it and even contemporary conclusions are difficult to test and confirm because the pace of change is so rapid and the record so limited.

[3] See Committee on Preservation of Historical Records (1986) especially pages 61-69. It was one of the first comprehensive attempts to address the problems associated the fragile character of information in electronic form. The focus was mainly on media, but the authors did recognise that "hardware will become obsolete within a couple of decades." Optimistic promises crept into the report; it was estimated that polyethylene terephthalate (PET) film would last 1000 years.

[4] See Ross 1993: 11. A similar argument could be made for digital film and audio because of their market penetration and the proven commercial value of historic recordings and the enduring interest in films.

[5] Nuclear Information and Records Management Association (NIRMA), <http://www.nirma.org>.

6 See Herbst & Malle 1995: 155-160. The Boeing 777 was designed entirely on computer. <http://www.boeing.com/news/releases/1995/news.release.950614-a.html> The design data will be required in processable form for the life of the product; in the evident of claims of design negligence it may be essential to be able to use the original processing software and hardware (or emulation) to verify that with the technology available to the designers they could not have seen phenomena that could be observed when newer tools are used to study the same design data.

7 The National Research Council (1995: 31) pointed out that much of the early Landsat imagery needed to be rescued before it could be made accessible but that the work was carried out because 'retrospective data are vital to understanding long-term changes in natural phenomena.' The power of time-series data of this kind in helping us to understand the impact we are having on our planet is exemplified by the case study of Rondônia (Brazil).
The deforestation can be seen by comparing images taken in 1975, 1986, and 1992, see <http://edcwww.cr.usgs.gov/earthshots/slow/Rondonia/Rondonia>. Another good case study is of the change in the Aral Sea between 1964 and 1997, <http://edcwww.cr.usgs.gov/earthshots/slow/Aral/Aral>.

8 <http://ssdoo.gsfc.nasa.gov/nost/isoas/us01/minutes.html> There are other cost models that suggest that annual storage costs are higher, but still lower than the costs associated with the re-creation of the resources. See for example Dollar 1999: 207-213. Modelling the costs of preservation of digital data remains an area where much more research needs to be carried out. See for instance National Preservation Office 1999; Feeney (ed.) 1999: 50-60.

9 Lubell 2000: 72-78. The quantities of data created through the digitisation or digital production of film are massive: to store the digital version of Star Wars Episode I required nineteen 18 GB hard drives and Toy Story covered more than 300GB of storage. The value though of the preservation of this material for long term access already has a proven business case.

10 While much of the large genera of web-based fiction that is emerging may be of limited merit it will still have an impact on the growth of net-books and web-fiction and as such may merit preservation. This is the experimental phase from which new genera will spring.

11 Bikson & Law 1993: 89-124; Samuels 1998: 101-119; Wallace 1998, <http://www.rbarry.com/dwallace.html>; ARMA 2000.

12 In the case of Armstrong v. Executive Office of the President Judge Richey ruled that email in digital form contained information (e.g. transmission and receipt data and links between the messages) that was not present in the printouts. Printed versions were not faithful to the original and were, therefore, no substitute for them, <http://www.eff.org/pub/Legal/Cases/Armstrong_v_President>. The principle is that information in electronic form contains details that when it is preserved in any other way than digitally become lost. It is worth remembering that even in contemporary contexts judges, jurors and lawyers like electronic mail because they believe that the contents of email reflect more accurately the true feelings of the author. A view enhanced by the generally informal character of email. Sipior & Ward (1999: 88-95) describe the dangers of unrestrained access to email can pose to institutions.

[13] Three examples come to mind: Le Roy Ladurie's *Montaillu* an ethnohistorical study of this Cathar village in South-western France based on the one surviving volume of the inquisition record for the village (1978); Jan Vansina's, studies of African history, which were built on oral histories recorded in African communities, and, Nancy Farriss' *Maya Society Under Colonial Rule: The Collective Enterprise of Survival* which investigates culture and cultural change (1984). The work of many other historians (e.g. Trevelyan, Marc Block, Thompson, Thomas, Duby, Braudel, and Le Goff) shows the diversity of approaches historians take when investigating the past.

[14] See Brosius 1996. The work altered our perception of women in the ancient near east: between 549 and 333 BC there is unequivocal evidence that some owned extensive estates and presided over great wealth, some were leaders of large workgroups, and they were remunerated equally with men for the same work. These records made it feasible to demonstrate the inadequacies of Herodotus' account.

[15] The Alberta Hail Project for instance transferred gigabytes of data from tape to CD-R, a medium which is widely recognised as unstable, see Kochtubajda, Humphrey & Johnson: 1995, <http://datalib.library.ualberta.ca/AHParchive/Archive.html>. On CDs see Ross & Gow 1999: 11-13; See Kim, Nam & Huh 1997: 88-92; Södergård, Martovaara, & Virtanen 1995. CD-Rs are susceptible to damage through exposure to light, heat, and dampness. Those CD-Rs with data receiving layers made with pthalocyanine rather than cyanine dyes are the more stable. The latter is an organic dye and the former is a metallic stabilised dye. CD-Rs tend to be more stable than CD-RWs. DVD (Digital Versatile Disk) and DVD-R have similar stability issues associated with them.

[16] Metadata are data that makes other data meaningful and usable.

[17] The carrier (e.g. cartridge, tape, or diskette) does contain markings which may provide an indication as to the media class, the device needed to read it and in turn the hardware and software on which it contents might be made accessible.

[18] The literature examining wear, decay through hydrolysis, loss of lubrication, the interaction of the chemicals in magnetic media and loss of magnetic properties is extensive. From among the numerous reports, the following four indicate the scale and diversity of the research into magnetic media: Kajdas & Bhusham 1999: 303-320; Nishida, Kikkawa & H. 1999: 2451-2453; Hempstock, Wild, Sullivan & Mayo 1998: 435-441; Gao 1998: 238-242. Some of these developments are very positive: early magnetic media (e.g. 1960-85) had low coercivity and as a result were susceptible to data loss from stray magnetic fields (e.g. magnets in motors such as those that drive the belts in airport security x-ray machines. For example, the coercivity of 720K 3.5" floppies was about 300 Oe, 1.44K 3.5" floppies 700 Oe, and Quarter-inch cartridge (QIC) tape (say the DC600A) rated 550Oe. Newer media has comparatively high coercivity and is as a result less susceptible to stray magnetism. Most media is now higher than 1000 Oe; hard-disc drives made during the 1990s had coercivities ranging between 1400 Oe and 2200 Oe. In the case of tapes, print-through, where the data from one layer is imprinted on the adjacent tape, remains a problem. Signal decay in magnetic media is much less of a problem than is the breakdown of the media binder itself.

[19] Newer systems and improved storage devices (e.g. tape drives, discs) lead businesses to replace peripheral devices often without copying older material that is no

longer in current use to the new devices. Without these older devices the media often proves unreadable when it is required for long term preservation or evidential purpose. See the Virtual Museum of Computing <http://vmoc.museophile.com>, the Computer Conservation Society <http://www.cs.man.ac.uk/CCS>, or Computer History <http://ei.cs.vt.edu/~history/machines.html> for examples of efforts to record maintain, and preserve computer technology. The accumulation of information about obsolete computers and the machines themselves has become a popular activity and the web is littered with sites describing growing public and private collections. See for instance <http://www.obsoletecomputermuseum.org> and from here it is possible to follow a webring to other sources.

[20] The layering of encoding plays a role in interpreting digital information. At the highest level in the hierarchy there is the file of a particular format and at the lowest there are the data as stored on the media itself. Data are encoded as magnetic domains on tapes and discs or as pits on optical media (CDs). The magnetic domains represent the 1s and 0s as written to the media by the write-heads. These 1s and 0s as stored on the raw media do not necessarily share a one-to-one correspondence with the contents of a particular file. For instance before the data was passed to the controller for writing it might have been compressed (say using LZW [Lempel-Ziv-Welch]) and then the controller itself might write other data before or after the bitstream to assist it to locate and track the data across the media (say in the case of tapes block headers). There are a number of ways of encoding data on to the surface of the media. For instance, Non-Return to Zero (NRZ) is simple way of recording data on to the magnetic surface. This represents 1 (one) bit by a change in magnetic polarity and a 0 (zero) by no change. Identifying the bit stream and retrieving the bit stream would only be the beginning of the problem. It is then necessary to determine what is encoded. Even for the encoding of text there were competing standards at one time, ASCII (American Standard Code for Information Interchange) and IBM's EBCDIC (Extended Binary Coded Decimal Information Code); and if the sequence of bits turned out to be an character and not a segment of an image it could be 7-bit or 8-bit ASCII or 8-bit EBCDIC. This is just the start.

[21] In the United States the Andrew W. Mellon Foundation and National Science Foundation Digital Libraries Programme and in the United Kingdom the Heritage Lottery Fund and the Joint Information Systems Committee are examples of active players. An increasing number of commercial firms, recognising the business potential of owning and delivering digital content, are developing digital stockpiles, including Corbis and Getty Images (see for instance, 'Blood and Oil', *The Economist*, 4 March 2000, 97). These resources enable new research (e.g. Shapiro 1998: 279-296).

[22] Commission on Preservation and Access 1993.

[23] Elsewhere I have argued that we need national strategies: *Funding Information and Communications Technology in the Heritage Sector*, Policy Recommendations to the Heritage Lottery Fund (January, 1998), see <http://www.hatii.arts.gla.ac.uk/HLFICT/cover3.html> or in the case of the European Union trans-country strategies to ensure that we invest in creating unique, interoperable, and consistent quality digital resources.

[24] The Beowulf Project has created a 'diplomatic edition' with transcription, translation and a wide range of additional resources to make this manuscript accessible to stu-

dents and scholars in a way that will make it possible for them to develop a fuller understanding of its creation, change over-time, and the tradition to which it belonged. See: Kiernan 1994: 15, <http://www.bl.uk/diglib/beowulf> or <http://www.uky.edu/~kiernan/welcome.html>; Prescott 1997: 185-195; Prescott 1998: 30-49.

[25] The Music Performance Research Centre has digitised 1800 musical performances captured during the last sixty-five years; a collection which in digital form truly enables performance studies (e.g. comparison of live and studio performances). Access to and use of MPRC recordings are restricted by the single issue, which will pose the major obstacle to the future of scholarship: intellectual property rights (IPR). Heritage Lottery Fund Project (DG-95-00980).

[26] Kenney 1996: 41-47. Kenney 1998, <http://www.library.cornell.edu/preservation/com/comfin.html>.

[27] Moffett 1992: 39-52. See also the Lexicon of Greek Personal Names (LGPN) Moffett 1996, <http://www.lgpn.ox.ac.uk/itindex.html>, which is providing scholars with the tools to reshape our knowledge about the Greek world.

[28] The SCAN project is digitising some 400,000 wills and testaments from the Middle Ages until the late 19th century a resource of some 3 million pages; a valuable starting point for research both by scholars and the general public, especially for genealogists who are among the largest users of archives. MacKenzie 1999: 139-149.

[29] Thomas, Alexander & Guthrie 1999: 60-65; see also <http://www.jstor.org>.

[30] <http://moa.umdl.umich.edu>.

[31] This project has made available the archives of a small German town.

[32] <http://www.aldus.unipr.it/tbd/digit.pdf>.

[33] Knowles 1963. Of course many of these products were themselves printed on acidic paper and are now the subject of retroconversion efforts. A benchmark study of the impact of computers on the humanities and social sciences is: Coppock (eds) 1999.

[34] <http://www.ornl.gov/TechResources/Human_Genome/home.html>. These databases themselves become the raw material for future researchers. For instance, Kasif (1999: 38-43) describes an approach for assisting in the discovery of 'the fundamental connections between genetic sequences and functions of living organisms.'

[35] Barker, Garavelli, Haft, Hunt, Marzec, Orcutt, Srinivasarao, Yeh, Ledley, Mewes, Pfeiffer & Tsugita 1998: 27-32. See also <http://www-nbrf.georgetown.edu>.

[36] Ross 1994: 629-635. CRSBI is creating a digital record with associated text-base of the 100,000 surviving examples of Romanesque sculpture in Britain and Ireland.

[37] Images of England is creating a digital image for each of the 360,000 listed structures in the England and linking them to the text-based database listed building record, <http://www.imagesofengland.org.uk>. The project, which will have cost more than four million pounds by the time it is finished in four years time, will provide public access to a national visual record of the listed buildings of England. This visual record will provide a benchmark for future study of our built heritage and help us to chart changes in it. It will itself be an important cultural resource.

38 <http://intarch.ac.uk Heyworth> Ross, & Richards 1996: 517-523, <http://intarch.ac.uk/news/caa95.htm> Ross 1999a: 316-317.

39 See Barry 1994: 251-256, <http://www.caldeson.com/RIMOS/barry1.html>.

40 Estimating the size of the Web environment is difficult. In its July 1999 Internet Domain Survey the Internet Software Consortium identified some 56.2 million Internet hosts. In 1999 Network Solutions registered roughly 5.3 million domain names.

41 In 1956 disk storage cost $200,000 a megabyte, by 1991 that cost had fallen to $5 a megabyte, and by 1998 it had plummeted to 5 cents a megabyte. The costs continue to fall, but storage brings with it numerous management costs.

42 Numerous contemporary mining examples using longitudinal data indicate the kinds of results that can be obtained. For instance Mackillop, Zhou, Groome, Dixon, Cummings, Hayter, & Paszat (1999: 355-362) used radiotherapy data collected over an eleven year period as part of the recordkeeping functions of hospitals to examine how its use had changed.

43 The 1999 DLM Forum set in motion a programme to raise awareness among the industrial and software development communities of these issues and to build collaborative initiatives, <http://www.dlmforum.eu.org>.

44 For example, Adams, Hansen, Walker & Gash (1998) reported on the systems they were developing to address the terabytes of data storage in multiple formats that scientists were generating in research laboratories they supported.

45 Macedonia 2000: 124-127. The relatively new gaming and edutainment sector employs 29% of the staff in motion picture business, yet it generates 79% of the revenues (*ib.*: 126).

46 Held in 1993 and sponsored by the British Academy, the British Library and the Association for History and Computing.

47 Burnet & Supnik (1996) note: 'The implementation of a particular simulator begins with collecting reference manuals, maintenance manuals, design documents, folklore, and prior simulator implementations for the target system. This is nontrivial. In the early days of computing, companies did not systematically collect and archive design documentation. In addition, collected material is subject to information decay, as noted earlier. Lastly, the material is likely to be contradictory, embodying differing revisions or versions of the architecture, as well as errors that have crept in during the documentation process."

48 In many ways even more worrying is the debate as to whether records should remain in the custody of their creating organisation or be transferred to archives. See the National Archives of Australia.

49 Ross 1998. See also Eastwood, Shadrack Katuu, Killawee & Whyte 1999: 277-300.

50 Not all digital resources will have their associated documentation in digital form (e.g. manuals). While it remains on paper it can easily be severed from the digital resources which it describes and is susceptible, even under optimal conditions, to loss. In order to mitigate against the loss of information that might occur if these documents

became unavailable, strategies and procedures will need to be established to ensure that they are converted into digital form. The research into the use of XML (see Usdin & Graham 1998: 125-132) to aid the preservation of digital resources is increasingly extensive: see for instance <http://www.icpsr.umich.edu/DDI/intro.html> or for the central place XML encoding of metadata in work of the Object Oriented Data Technology (OODT) group which carries out research into object oriented data systems technologies for Section 389, JPL, and NASA. Their report *Object Oriented Data Technology for Interferometry Systems* <http://oodt.jpl.nasa.gov/doc/reports/annual/1999> provides an example of the key role that XML can play in preservation and access strategies. Currently the conversion to eXtensible Markup Language (XML) offers the best preservation option. Where it proves impossible to convert this material into XML format the preferred digital format for these materials should be Tagged Interchange File Format (TIFF), which is recognised as a preservation standard.

[51] There are a number of excellent bibliographic sources, including: (1) Preserving Access to Digital Information, <http://www.nla.gov.au/padi> (2) United Kingdom Office for Library Networking, <http://homes.ukoln.ac.uk/~lismd/preservation.html> (3) the University of Pittsburgh Functional Requirements Project, <http://www.lis.pitt.edu/~nhprc/bibtc.html> (4) the InterPARES project-American Team, <http://is.gseis.ucla.edu/us-interpares/bibgraph.htm>.

[52] See for instance Van der Werf-Davelaar, 'NEDLIB: Networked European Deposit Library', <http://www.exploit-lib.org/issue4/nedlib> or the NEDLIB site itself, <http://www.konbib.nl/nedlib>.

[53] The InterPARES Project, <http://www.interpares.org>; Kristine L. Kelly, Alan Kowlowitz, Theresa A. Pardo, and Darryl E. Green, *Models for Action: Practical Approaches to Electronic Records Management & Preservation*, (Albany, CTG Final Project Report CTG 98-1) July 1998, <http://www.ctg.albany.edu/resources/pdfrp-wp/mfa.pdf>. There are numerous other initiatives such as the European Commission funded work on functional requirements for metadata and work at pharmaceutical companies such as Pfizer and Astra.

[54] A search of the web produces many computer preservation groups, museums and research projects. See also Roger Bridgman, 'What's in a Computer?', Suzanne Keene and Doron Swade (eds), *Collecting and Conserving Computers*, (London: The National Museum of Science and Industry, 1994), 7-18. In its 1986 report the Committee on Preservation of Historical Records noted: 'Moreover it must be realised that no archival organisation can hope realistically to maintain such hardware itself. Integrated circuits, thin film heads, and laser diodes cannot be repaired today, nor can they be readily fabricated, except in multimillion-dollar factories' (page 68). There is one area where preservation of hardware is essential and this is the case of peripheral devices. While it is relatively simple to write a device driver to connect a peripheral device to computer it is much more difficult to build a tape or disk reader from scratch.

[55] Margaret Hedstrom, 'Research Issues in Migration and Long-Term Preservation,' *Archives and Museum Informatics* 11 (1997), 287-291.

[56] See Ross & Gow 1999: 27-36, <http://www.hatii.arts.gla.ac.uk/Projects/BrLibrary/index.html>.

⁵⁷ See British Standards Institution (99/621800 DC), *Bundles for the perpetual preservation of electronic documents and associated objects.*

⁵⁸ Moore, Baru, Gupta, Ludaescher, Marciano & Rajasekar 1999, <http://www.sdsc.edu/NARA/Publications/nara.pdf/>.

⁵⁹ Ross & Gow 1999: 37-38; Cifuentes & Van Emmerik 2000: 60; Cifuentes & Malhotra 1996: 340-349.

⁶⁰ This is not primarily because of media unreliability, because, as Ross & Gow 1999 have noted, magnetic media is durable even under extreme conditions. Although media decays and because of particle breakdown loses its signal, the main long-term difficulty is likely to be peripheral device obsolescence.

⁶¹ For instance Thibodeau (1999) has argued that NARA is now in a position to accession successfully substantial record collections (e.g. one million diplomatic records annually and 25 million messages from the Clinton administration). Moore, Baru, Rajasekar, Ludaescher, Marciano, Wan, Schroeder & Gupta 2000a, >. Moore, Baru, Rajasekar, Ludaescher, Marciano, Wan, Schroeder & Gupta 2000b, <http://www.dlib.org/dlib/april00/moore/04moore-pt2.html>.

⁶² See note 2 above.

⁶³ National Library of Australia 1999, <http://www.nla.gov.au/preserve/pmeta.html> or National Archives of Australia 1999, <http://www.naa.gov.au>. Reed 1997: 218-41; See also the summary of the Third Metadata Workshop <http://www.cordis.lu/libraries/en/metadata/metadata3.html>. Day & Stone 1999, <http://www.ariadne.ac.uk/issue20/metadata>.

⁶⁴ For instance the work in digital preservation metadata, *Metadata Specifications Derived from the Functional Requirements: A Reference Model for Business Acceptable Communications*, 9/18/96, (Functional Requirements for Evidence in Recordkeeping: The Pittsburgh Project), was never comprehensively tested. However the issues it tackled and how it tackled them have shaped much subsequent work in preservation metadata in the archives and libraries areas.

⁶⁵ See Ross 1995.

⁶⁶ Woodyard 1998, at the National Library of Australia website: <http://www.nla.gov.au/nla/staffpaper/valadw.html>. The handcrafted nature of migration is abundantly clear from Woodyard's work.

⁶⁷ Two very simple examples might help: (1) I have files that began life on a Morrow Computer running CP/M in Wordstar (1982), that were moved to an IBM compatible computer running Wordstar for DOS (1985), eventually moved to WordPerfect for DOS (1989), then to WordPerfect for Windows (1993), and then through a variety of Microsoft Word for Windows formats (beginning in 1997), but which remain accessible today (2000). (2) Of course dynamic documents created in Word 6 which included references to Word macros failed to migrate successfully to Word97. The migrated files no longer display origination (e.g. letterhead) data as this only existed in the macro and was instantiated at runtime and Microsoft changed the macro language from one version of Word to the next.

[68] When such loss occurs it needs to be documented. Inclusion of metadata describing change history forms a critical element in any preservation strategy.

[69] Among the current competing preservation metadata models the Cedars model shows promise, <http://www.leeds.ac.uk/cedars>. The use of repositories is a proven strategy and has been adopted, for instance, by the Library of Congress and NARA.

[70] CCSDS 650.0-R-1: *Reference Model for an Open Archival Information System (OAIS)*. Red Book. Issue 1. May 1999, <http://ssdoo.gsfc.nasa.gov/nost/isoas/ref_model.html>. In order to take advantage of the preservation strengths of the model it is essential that appropriate documentation and metadata standards be adopted. This information must be linked or wrapped round the resources themselves and be encoded in a functional and secure standard. A strategy of this kind ensures that the platform is in place to permit the application of best preservation strategy, whether that is migration, persistent objects or emulation to each digital resource. The focus of this strategy is on flexibility and responsiveness to changing conditions. Holdsworth & Sargent 2000, <http://gps0.leeds.ac.uk/~ecldh/cedars/nasa2000/nasa2000.html> demonstrates how the model might work.

[71] Rothenberg 1995: 24-29; Swade 1993: 93-104; Ross 1998: 6-28.

[72] Lorenzo Valla, *De falso credita et ementita Constantini donatione declamatio*, Mainz, 1518. Others had suspected and argued this was the case.

[73] See for instance, Kelly: 161-176.

[74] Small (1997) built some of her arguments on how the environment, materials (e.g. scrolls) and even the desk conditioned ancient thought.

[75] Ross & Gow 1999: 27-36. There are numerous emulators being developed see for example:
<http://ei.cs.vt.edu/~history/emulators.html> <http://www.chac.org/chhistpg.html>.

[76] Van Der Spiegel 1996, <http://www.upenn.edu/computing/printout/archive/v12/4/chip.html> and <http://www.ee.upenn.edu/~jan/eniacproj.html>.

[77] There are many emulators for the PDP-11. These include Software Resources International (SRI), CHARON-11 <http://www.charon-11.com>, of Ersatz-11, a software PDP-11 emulator for MS-DOS PCs <http://www.dbit.com>. These emulators support a wide range of device drivers.

[78] <http://www.dcs.warwick.ac.uk/~edsac>.

[79] Ross & Gow 1999: 24-25. Rugar, Mamin, Guethner, Lambert, Stren, McFadyen & Yogi 1990. Sáenz, García, Grutter, Meyer, Heinzelmann, Wiesendanger, Rosenthaler, Hidber & Gütherodt 1987. Recent articles (such as Arnett, Minvielle & Nair 1999: 479-483) indicate the potential of MFM. Boyd & Xu: 53-64.

[80] McClure & Sprehe 1998, <http://istweb.syr.edu/~mcclure/nhprc/nhprc_title.html>.

[81] Indeed the NASA adopted the view that 'because all e-mail can be the target of a number of public and legal disclosure instruments, and as the government's definition of 'records' is difficult to interpret and this policy is difficult to enforce, the agency has stipulated that all email files (central store only) that are older than 60 days must be erased automatically.' (Harreld 1997, <http://www.fcw.com/fcw/articles/1997/FCW_060297_487.asp>).

[82] We should not be tricked into believing that the survival of vast quantities of data will alone provide the fertile soil for future scholarship; research 50 years from now will be very different. The quality of the data (whether texts, multimedia, databases, or audio), the training of scholars, and the tools to investigate the data will each continue to influence the products of research.

[83] In 1999 the Joint Information Systems Committee (UK) released a CD-ROM titled, *Advisory Group on Computer Graphics: Reports and Resources Archive*. Shortly after receiving the CD a note followed saying that 'a virus has accidentally been included'. Although the virus does not have a 'destructive payload' it is easy to imagine the dangers that will lurk in the records that we pass to the future.

References

AA.VV.
1996 *Metadata Specifications Derived from the Functional Requirements: A Reference Model for Business Acceptable Communications*, 9/18/96, (Functional Requirements for Evidence in Recordkeeping: The Pittsburgh Project), <http://www.lis.pitt.edu/~nhprc/meta96.html>

ADAMS, D.R., D.M. HANSEN, K.G. WALKER & J.D. GASH
1998 "Scientific Data Archive at the Environmental Molecular Sciences Laboratory", *Sixth NASA Goddard Space Flight Center Conference on Mass Storage Systems and Technologies and Fifteenth IEEE Symposium on Mass Storage Systems*, March 23-26.

ARMA INTERNATIONAL STANDARDS COMMITTEE E-MAIL TASK FORCE
2000 *Guideline for Managing E-mail*.

ARNETT, P., T. MINVIELLE & S. NAIR
1998 "Extracting media noise characteristics from MFM images", *Journal of Magnetism and Magnetic Materials*, 193.1-3: 479-483.

AUBERT, J-J.
1994 *Business Managers in Ancient Rome: A Social and Economic Study of Institores, 200 B.C.-A.D. 250*, Leiden: E.J. Brill.

BARKER, W.C., ET. AL.
1998 "The PIR-International Protein Sequence Database", *Nucleic Acids Research*, 26.1: 27-32.

BARRY, R.E.
1994 "Electronic document and records management systems: Towards a methodology for requirements definitions", *Information Management and Technology*, 27.6: 251-256.

BHUSHAN, B. & R.M. PHELAN
1987 "Overview of Challenger Space-Shuttle Tape-Data Recovery Study", *IEEE Transactions on Magnetics*, 23.5: 3179-3183.

BIKSON, T.K. & S.A. LAW
1993 "Electronic mail use at the World Bank: Messages from users", *The Information Society* 9.2: 89-124.

BOYD, M. & XU, X.
"MR glide inspection for hard disk defect detection", *Proceedings of SPIE - The International Society for Optical Engineering*, 3619: 53-64.

BRIDGMAN, R.
1994 "What's in a Computer?", in S. Keene & D. Swade (eds.), *Collecting and Conserving Computers*, London: The National Museum of Science and Industry: 7-18.

BRITISH STANDARDS INSTITUTION
Bundles for the Perpetual Preservation of Electronic Documents and Associated Objects, 99/621800 DC.

BROSIUS, M.
1996 *Women in Ancient Persia*, Oxford: Oxford University Press.

BURNET, M.M. & R.M. SUPNIK
1996 "Preserving computing's past: Restoration and simulation", *Digital Technical Journal*, 8.3 <http://www.digital.com/info/DTJN02>

CATHALY, G.
1998 "Mass digitisation production chain at the Bibliothèque Nationale de France", *Digitisation of Library Materials: Report of the Concentration Meeting & Workshop*, Luxembourg, 14.12.98: 15- 19.

CCSDS
1999 650.0-R-1: *Reference Model for an Open Archival Information System (OAIS)*, Red Book, Issue 1, May 1999,
<http://ssdoo.gsfc.nasa.gov/nost/isoas/ref_model.html.>

CIFUENTES, C. & V. MALHOTRA
1996 "Binary translation: static, dynamic, retargetable?", *Proceedings of the 1996 IEEE Conference on Software Maintenance*: 340-349.

CIFUENTES, C. & M. VAN EMMERIK
2000 "UQBT: Adaptable binary translation at low cost", *Computer*, 33.3.

COMMISSION ON PRESERVATION AND ACCESS
1993 *Preserving the Intellectual Heritage: A Report of the Bellagio Conference*, June 7-10, Washington D.C.

COMMITTEE ON PRESERVATION OF HISTORICAL RECORDS
1986 *Preservation of Historical Records*, Washington D.C.: National Academy Press.

COPPOCK, T. (ED.)
1999 *Information Technology and Scholarship: Applications in the Humanities and Social Sciences*, Oxford: The British Academy.

DAY, M. & A. STONE
1999 "Metadata: The Third Luxembourg Metadata Workshop", *Ariadne*, 20, <http://www.ariadne.ac.uk/issue20/metadata>

DERY, M.
1996 *Escape Velocity: Cyberculture at the End of the Century*, New York: Grove/Atlantic.

DOLLAR, C.M.
1999 *Authentic Electronic Records: Strategies for Long-Term Access*, Chicago.

EASTWOOD, T. S. KATUU, J. KILLAWEE, & J.WHYTE
1999 "Appraisal of electronic records", in M. Guercio (ed.), *Archivi per la Storia, Rivista dell'Associazione Nazionale Archivistica Italiana*: 277-300.

EBELING, H.H. & M. THALLER (EDS.)
1999 *Digitale Archive: Die Erschließung und Digitalisierung des Stadtarchives Duderstadt*, Göttingen: Max-Planck-Institut für Geschichte.

FARRISS, N.
1984 *Maya Society Under Colonial Rule: The Collective Enterprise of Survival*.

GAO, C.
1998 "Corrosion evaluation of cobalt based magnetic films using various techniques', *Materials Research Innovations*, 1.4: 238-242.

GONZÁLEZ, P.
1999 *Computerization of the Archivo General de Indias: Strategies and Results*, Washington, D.C: CLIR publication 76.

HAN, J.
1998 "Towards on-line analytical mining in large datasets", *ACM SIGMOD Record* (March): 97-107.

HARRELD, H.
1997 "NASA orders all email destroyed", *Federal Computer Week*, 6/2/97. <http://www.fcw.com/fcw/articles/1997/FCW_060297_487.asp>

HEDSTROM, M.
1997 "Research issues in migration and long-term preservation", *Archives and Museum Informatics* 11: 287-291.

HEMPSTOCK, M.S., M.A. WILD, J.L. SULLIVAN & P.I. MAYO
1998 "A study of the durability of flexible magnetic media in a linear tape system", *Tribology*, 31.8: 435-441.

HENDLEY, T.
1998 *Comparison of Methods and Costs of Digital Preservation*, London: The British Library.

HERBST, A. & B. MALLE
1995 "Electronic archiving in the light of product liability", *KnowRight '95,* Vienna: Oldenbourg Verlag: 155-160.

HEYWORTH, M., S. ROSS & J. RICHARDS
1996 "Internet archaeology: An electronic journal for archaeology", in H. Kammermanns (ed.), *Interfacing the Past. Computer Applications and Quantitative Methods in Archaeology,* CAA95, in *Analecta Praehistorica Leidensia*, no. 28. (Leiden): 517-523, <http://intarch.ac.uk/news/caa95.htm>

HOLDSWORTH, D. & D.M. SARGENT
2000 *A Blueprint for Representation Information in the OAIS Model*, <http://gps0.leeds.ac.uk/~ecldh/cedars/nasa2000/nasa2000.html>

JONES, S.
1997 *Virtual Culture: Identity and Communication in Cybersociety*, London: Sage Publications.

JPL & NASA
1999 *Object Oriented Data Technology for Interferometry Systems,* <http://oodt.jpl.nasa.gov/doc/reports/annual/1999>

KAJDAS, C. & B. BHUSHAM
1999 "Mechanism of interaction and degradation of perfluoropolyethers with a DLC coating in thin-film magnetic rigid disks: A critical review", *Journal of Information Storage and Processing Systems*, 1.4: 303-320.

KALTHOFF, C.H., R.L. BRADSHAW, E.A. BARTKUS & B.I. FINKELSTEIN
1987 "Magnetic-Tape Recovery And Rerecording Of Data", *Journal of Applied Physics,* 61.8, 4004-6.

KASIF, S.
1999 "Datascope: Mining Biological Sequences", *IEEE Intelligent Systems*, 14.6: 38-43.

KELLY, C.M.
1994 "Later Roman bureaucracy: going through the files", in A.K. Bowman & G. Wolf (eds) *Literacy and Power in the Ancient World*, Cambridge: 161-176.

KENNEY, A.R.
1996 "Conversion of traditional source materials into digital form' in D. Bearman (ed.) *Research Agenda for Networked Cultural Heritage*, Santa Monica: Getty Art History Information Program: 41-47.

KENNEY, A.R.
1998 *Digital to Microfilm Conversion: A Demonstration Project 1994-1996, Final Report to the National Endowment for the Humanities* PS-20781-94. <http://www.library.cornell.edu/preservation/com/comfin.html>

KIERNAN, K.
1994 "Digital preservation, restoration, and dissemination of medieval manuscripts", in A. Oakerson (ed), *Scholarly Publishing on the Electronic Networks*, Proceedings of the Third Symposium, Washington D.C.: ARL Publications: 15, <http://www.bl.uk/diglib/beowulf> or <http://www.uky.edu/~kiernan/welcome.html>

KIM, J.S., T.Y. NAM & Y.J. HUH
1997 'The optical characteristics in the Layers of Compact Disc-Recordable", *Korean Journal of Chemical Engineering*, 14.2: 88-92.

KNOWLES, D.
1963 *Great Historical Enterprises*, London: Thomas Nelson & Sons Ltd.

KOCHTUBAJDA, B., C. HUMPHREY & M. JOHNSON
1995 *Data Rescue: Experiences from the Alberta Hail Project*, paper presented at the 21st Annual Conference of the International Association for Social Science Information Service and Technology 95 May 9-12, 1995, Quebec City, <http://datalib.library.ualberta.ca/AHParchive/Archive.html>

KRISTINE L.K., A. KOWLOWITZ, TH.A. PARDO & D.E. GREEN
1998 *Models for Action: Practical Approaches to Electronic Records Management & Preservation*, Albany, CTG Final Project Report CTG 98-1, July 1998. <http://www.ctg.albany.edu/resources/pdfrpwp/mfa.pdf>

LE ROY LADURIE, E.
1978 *Montaillu*

LORD, P.
1997 "Strategies and tactics for managing electronic data records: A view from the pharmaceutical industry", *INSAR (Supplement II), Proceedings of the DLM-Forum on electronic records*: 168-174.

LUBELL, P.D.
2000 "A coming attraction D-Cinema", *Spectrum*, 37.3, March 2000: 72-78.

MACEDONIA, M.
2000 "Why Digital Entertainment Drives the Need for Speed", *Computer*, 33.2: 124-127.

MACFARLANE, I.
1998 "Electronic records management systems, a report from the Working Group", *Electronic Access: Archives in the New Millennium*, Proceedings, 3-4 June 1998, London: Public Record Office: 70-73.

MACKENZIE, G.
1999 "Digitising the Scottish Wills", in T. Coppock (ed.), *Making Information Available in Digital Format: Perspectives from Practitioners*, Edinburgh: The Stationery Office: 139-149.

MACKILLOP, W.J., S. ZHOU, P. GROOME, P. DIXON, B.J. CUMMINGS, C. HAYTER, & L. PASZAT
1999 "Changes in the use of radiotherapy in Ontario 1984-1995", *International Journal of Radiation Oncology Biology Physics*, 44.2: 355-362.

MAES, P.
1994 "Agents that reduce work and information overload", *Communications of the ACM*, 37.7: 30-40.

MCCLURE, C.R. & J.T.SPREHE
1998 *Analysis and Development of Model Quality Guidelines for Electronic Records Management on State and Federal Websites. Final Report*, January 1998. <http://istweb.syr.edu/~mcclure/nhprc/nhprc_title.html>

MLADENIC, D.
1999 "Text-learning and related intelligent agents: A survey", *IEEE Intelligent Systems*, 14.4: 44-54.

MOFFETT, J.C.
1992 "The Beazley Archive – Making a humanities database accessible to the world", *Bulletin of The John Rylands University Library of Manchester*, 74.3: 39-52.
1996 *A Case of Data Metamorphosis: A Description of the Computerization of LGPN Data*, <http://www.lgpn.ox.ac.uk/itindex.html>

MOORE, R. C. BARU, A. RAJASEKAR, B. LUDAESCHER, R. MARCIANO, M. WAN, W. SCHROEDER & A. GUPTA.
2000a "Collection-based persistent digital archives – Part 1", *D-Lib Magazine* 6.3: March 2000 ISSN 1082-9873,
<http://www.dlib.org/dlib/march00/moore/03moore-pt1.html>
2000b "Collection-based persistent digital archives – Part 2", *D-Lib Magazine* 6.4: April 2000 ISSN 1082-9873 <http://www.dlib.org/dlib/april00/moore/04moore-pt2.html>

MOORE, R., C. BARU, A. GUPTA, B. LUDAESCHER, R. MARCIANO & A. RAJASEKAR
1999 *Collection-Based Long-Term Preservation*, San Diego: Computer Center, San Diego, <http://www.sdsc.edu/NARA/Publications/nara.pdf>

NATIONAL ARCHIVES OF AUSTRALIA
1999 *Recordkeeping Metadata Standard for Commonwealth Agencies*. Version 1.0. May 1999. <http://www.naa.gov.au/govserv/techpub/rkms/intro.htm>
National Library of Australia, Preservation Metadata for Digital Collections, 15 October 1999, <http://www.nla.gov.au/preserve/pmeta.html>

NATIONAL PRESERVATION OFFICE
1999 *Digital Culture: Maximising the Nation's Investment: A Synthesis of JISC/NPO Studies on the Preservation of Electronic Materials*, M. Feeney (ed), London: The National Preservation Office, The British Library.

NATIONAL RESEARCH COUNCIL
1995 *Preserving Scientific Data on Our Physical Universe: A New Strategy for Archiving the Nation's Scientific Information Resources,* Washington D.C.: National Academy Press.

NISHIDA, Y., M. KIKKAWA & H. KONDO
1999 "Behavior of lubricant migration in particulate magnetic recording media", *IEEE Transactions on Magnetics*, 35.5: 2451-2453.

NUCLEAR INFORMATION AND RECORDS MANAGEMENT ASSOCIATION (NIRMA)
<http://www.nirma.org/newhome>

PORTER, D.
1997 *Internet Culture,* London: Routledge.

PRESCOTT, A.
1997 "The electronic *Beowulf* and digital restoration", *Literary and Linguistic Computing,* 12.3: 185-195.
1998 "Constructing Electronic *Beowulf*", in L. Carpenter, S. Shaw & A. Prescott (eds.), *Towards the Digital Library: The British Library's 'Initiatives for Access' Programme,* London: The British Library: 30-49.

PYLE, D.
1999 *Data Preparation for Data Mining,* San Mateo (CA): Morgan Kaufmann.

REED, B.
1997 "Metadata: Core record or core business?", *Archives and Manuscripts,* 25.2: 218-41.

RHEINGOLD, H.
1995 *The Virtual Community: Homesteading on the Electronic Frontier,* London.

ROBERTSON, S.B.
1996 *Digital Rosetta Stone: A Conceptual Model for Maintaining Long-term Access to Digital Documents.* Thesis (MSc), Air Force Institute of Technology, Graduate School of Logistics and Acquisition Management, <http://www.au.af.mil/au>

ROSS, S.
1993 "Historians, machine-readable information and the past's future", in S. Ross & E. Higgs (eds), *Electronic Information Resources and Historians: European Perspectives,* St Katharinen.
1994 "Designing a tool for research in disciplines using multimedia data: The Romanesque sculpture processor", in F. Bocchi & P. Denley (eds.), *Storia & Multimedia,* Proceedings of the Seventh International Congress of the Association for History and Computing, Bologna 29.8-2.9.1992, Bologna: 629-635.
1995 "Commentary on the Pittsburgh University The Record keeping Functional Requirements Project: A Progress Report', *The Society of American Archivists 1995 Conference,* Washington D.C. August 31 1995.
<http://www.hatii.arts.gla.ac.uk/sross/saa1995.html>.
1997 "Consensus, communication, and collaboration: fostering multidisciplinary cooperation in electronic records", in *INSAR (Supplement II), Proceedings of the DLM-Forum on electronic records*: 330-336.
1998a "Responding to the challenges and opportunities of ICT: The New Records Manager", A. Allen (eds), *Professionalism Plus,* Business Archives Council, Proceedings of the Annual Conference: 9-25.
1998b 'The expanding world of electronic information and the past's future', in E. Higgs (ed.), *Historians and Electronic Artefacts,* Oxford: Oxford University Press: 6-28.

1998c *Funding Information and Communications Technology in the Heritage Sector,* Policy Recommendations to the Heritage Lottery Fund (January, 1998) <http://www.arts.gla.ac.uk/HATII/HLFICT>

1999 "Preservation and Networking in Aid of Research", in T. Coppock (ed.), *Information Technology and Scholarship: Applications in the Humanities and Social Sciences,* Oxford: Oxford University Press: 316-317.

1999 'Strategies for selecting resources for digitisation: source-orientated, user-driven, asset-aware model (SOUDAAM)', in T. Coppock (ed.), *Making Information Available in Digital Format: Perspectives from Practitioners,* Edinburgh: The Stationery Office: 5-27.

Ross, S. & A. Gow
1999 *Digital Archaeology: Rescuing Neglected and Damaged Data Resources,* London.

Rothenberg, J.
1995 "Ensuring the longevity of digital documents", *Scientific American,* 272, 1 January 1995: 24-29

Rugar, D., H.J. Mamin, P. Guethner, S.E. Lambert, J.E. Stren, I. McFadyen & T. Yogi
1990 "Magnetic force microscopy: General principles and application to longitudinal recording media", *Journal of Applied Physics:* 68.3.

Sáenz, J.J., N. García, P. Grutter, E. Meyer, H. Heinzelmann, R. Wiesendanger, L. Rosenthaler, H.R. Hidber, & H.-J. Gütherodt
1987 "Observations of magnetic forces by the atomic force microscope", *Journal of Applied Physics:* 62.10.

Samuels, J.
1998 "Electronic mail: Information exchange or information loss?", in E. Higgs (ed.), *Historians and Electronic Artefacts,* Oxford: Oxford University Press.

Shapiro, F.R.,
1998 "A study in computer-assisted lexicology: Evidence on the emergence of hopefully as a sentence adverb from the JSTOR journal archive and other electronic resources', *American Speech,* 73.3: 279-296.

Shulman, S.
1999 *Owing the Future,* Boston: Houghton Mifflin Co.

Sipior, J.C. & B.T. Ward
1999 "The dark side of employee e-mail", *Communications of the ACM,* 42.7, 1999: 88-95.

Small, J.P.
1997 *Wax Tablets of the Mind Cognitive Studies of Memory and Literacy in Classical Antiquity:* Routledge.

Södergård, C., Martovaara, J. & J. Virtanen
1995 *Research on the Life Expectancy of the CD-R (CD-R levyjen säilytyskestävyyden tutkiminen. Undersökning av CD-R skivors beständighet)* (Helsinki).

STUCKEY, S.
"The Good Oil for Australia": 97-100.

SWADE, D.,
1993 "Collecting software: Preserving information in an object-centred culture", in S. Ross & E. Higgs (eds.), *Electronic Information Resources and Historians: European Perspectives*, St Katharinen: Scripta Mercaturae Verlag: 93-104

THIBODEAU, K.
1999 *Persistent Object Preservation: Advanced Computing Infrastructure for Digital Preservation*, DLM-Forum.

THOMAS, S.W., ALEXANDER, K. & K. GUTHRIE
1999 "Technology choices for JSTOR online archive", *Computer*, February 1999: 60-65.

TURKLE, S.
1997 *Life on the Screen*, New York: Simon & Schuster.

USDIN, T. & GRAHAM, T.
1998 "XML: Not a silver bullet, but a great pipe wrench", *StandardView*, 6.3: 125-132.

VALLA, L.
1518 *De falso credita et ementita Constantini donatione declamatio*, Mainz.

VAN DER SPIEGEL, J.
1996 "ENIAC-on-a-Chip", *PennPrintout*, 12.4 (March 1996), <http://www.upenn.edu/computing/printout/archive/v12/4/chip.html> and <http://www.ee.upenn.edu/~jan/eniacproj.html>

VAN DER WERF-DAVELAAR, T.
2000 "NEDLIB: Networked European Deposit Library".

WALLACE, D.A.
1998 *Recordkeeping and Electronic Mail Policy: The State of Thought and the State of the Practice*, <http://www.rbarry.com/dwallace.html>

WETTENGEL, M.
1998 "German Unification and Electronic Records", E. Higgs (ed), *History and Electronic Artefacts*, Oxford: Clarendon Press: 264-276.

WOODYARD, D.
1998 *Farewell my Floppy: A Strategy for Migration of Digital Information*, at the National Library of Australia website:
<http://www.nla.gov.au/nla/staffpaper/valadw.html>